FRONTIERS OF KNOWLEDGE

A RESEARCH FRAMEWORK FOR HADRIAN'S WALL, PART OF THE FRONTIERS OF THE ROMAN EMPIRE WORLD HERITAGE SITE

VOLUME II AGENDA AND STRATEGY

Edited by:
Matthew F A Symonds & David J P Mason

from contributions by:-
Lindsay Allason-Jones, Paul Austen, Justine Bayley, Paul Bidwell, Andrew Birley, Robin Birley, Mike Bishop, David Breeze, Richard Brickstock, Ian Caruana, Mike Collins, Robert Collins, Jim Crow, Tim Gates, Elizabeth Greene, Kaye Hartley, Mark Hassall, Martin Henig, Peter Hill, Richard Hingley, Nick Hodgson, Jacqui Huntley, Rachael Newman, Tim Padley, John Pearce, David Petts, John Poulter, Jenny Price, Margaret Snape, Graeme Stobbs, John Shipley, Sue Stallibrass, Vivien Swan*, Jane Webster, Humphrey Welfare, Tony Wilmott, Steve Willis, David Woolliscroft, Robert Young and John Zant

Bust of Hadrian by M Buonarroti. Corbridge Museum, reproduced by kind permission of English Heritage

Contents

List of Illustrations

Tables

The authors are extremely grateful to the institutions and individuals listed below who have given their permission for the reproduction of images in their ownership.

Cumberland & Westmorland Archaeological & Architectural Society: 168, 204
Cumbria County Council: 44
English Heritage: 13, 17, 18, 24
Mark Repath: 19
Museum of Antiquities, Newcastle upon Tyne: 48
Oxford Archaeology (North): 33
Society of Antiquaries of Newcastle upon Tyne: 2, 3, 31, 43
Tyne & Wear Museums: 15, 20, 23, 25, 35, 42
The Vindolanda Trust: 49
Tim Gates: 34, 38
Matthew Symonds: 4, 5, 6, 7, 8, 9, 10, 11, 12, 14, 16, 21, 22, 26, 27, 29, 30, 36, 39, 40, 41, 45, 46, 47, 50, 51, 52.

Abbreviations

AHRC: Arts and Humanities Research Council

ALSF: Aggregates Levy Sustainability Fund

C14: Carbon 14

CSIR: *Corpus Signorum Imperii Romani*, Corpus of Sculpture of the Roman World. 1977- published by Oxford University Press for The British Academy.

EDXRF: Energy Dispersive X-ray Fluorescence

GIS: Geographical Information System

HE: Historic Environment

LiDAR: Light detection and ranging, an optical remote sensing technique

LPRIA: Late pre-Roman Iron Age

NERRF: The North East Regional Research Framework (Petts 2006)

NMP: The National Mapping Programme

NWRRF: The North West Regional Research Framework (Brennand 2006; Brennand and Chitty 2007)

RIB: Collingwood, R G & Wright R P 1965. The Roman Inscriptions of Britain:I. Inscriptions on Stone, Oxford. (reprinted with *addenda* and *corrigenda* in 1995 by R S O Tomlin).

PPG16: Planning Policy Guidance 16, covering the Secretary of State's policy on archaeological remains on land

TW: An abbreviation of Turf Wall, used to distinguish between milecastles built to the Turf Wall specifications and their Stone Wall replacements

WHS: The World Heritage Site of Hadrian's Wall

Acknowledgements

This project has relied upon voluntary contributions from a large number of archaeologists working on Hadrian's Wall issues and we are very grateful to all those who have given freely of their time and expertise in order to produce this research framework. As well as producing the summaries of current knowledge that make up the Assessment section of the framework, 49 individuals attended one or more of the three public seminar days devoted to devising the Research Agenda and Strategy. Representing a range of organisations and viewpoints, it is thanks to the engagement of the archaeological community and the support of bodies that allowed them to contribute that the creation of this document has been possible. The project was funded by English Heritage and facilitated by Durham County Council and Archaeological Services, Durham University. Peter Carne of the latter institution was co-manager for the project. This role subsequently passed to David Petts, originally the Project Officer for the Research Framework, on his return to Durham University following a brief sojourn at Chester University. Matthew Symonds took over from David Petts as Project Officer at the stage when the Assessment phase was nearing completion.

Particular thanks are due to the Steering group, chaired by David Breeze, for their help, guidance and advice. As well as agreeing the structure and methodology of the project, they provided valuable feedback on early drafts of the text. The members were Lindsay Allason-Jones, Paul Austen, Paul Bidwell, Andrew Birley, Colin Burgess, Mike Collins, Jim Crow, Jacqui Huntley, David Miles, Rachel Newman, Richard Newman, Tim Padley, Kathy Perrin, Sarah Rushton, Tony Wilmott, Pete Wilson and Rob Young.

The eight thematic groups were co-ordinated respectively by Matthew Symonds with Rob Young, Nick Hodgson, Paul Bidwell with Peter Hill, David Mason with Jim Crow, Jacqui Huntley with Sue Stallibrass, Richard Hingley with Lindsay Allason-Jones, Jenny Price with Daniel Robinson and later David Petts and Tony Wilmott with Colm O'Brien. As well as delivering the text for the Assessment, many of the coordinators led the discussion of their themes at the three seminar days. The project is also grateful to Rachel Newman, Margaret Snape and Humphrey Welfare for leading thematic discussion at the seminar days and David Breeze for chairing them. Thanks are also owed to those not mentioned hitherto who contributed to discussions at the seminars and/or submitted comments electronically: Alan Biggins, Patricia Birley, Yvonne Boutwood, Mark Brennand, James Bruhn, Alex Croom, Ian Haynes, Birgitta Hoffman, Fraser Hunter, Valerie Maxfield, Georgina Plowright, Daniel Robinson and David Shotter.

We are grateful to the Society of Antiquaries of Newcastle-upon-Tyne, The Cumberland and Westmorland Antiquarian and Archaeological Society, Tyne and Wear Museums Service, The Vindolanda Trust, The Museum of Antiquities, Cumbria County Council, English Heritage, Tim Gates, David Woolliscroft and David J. Breeze for permission to reproduce their illustrations within the text.

Finally we would like to thank all of the many individuals who downloaded the project documents from the website and gave us their observations.

David JP Mason

RESEARCH AGENDA

Introduction

In this section, key gaps in knowledge pertaining to our understanding of the eight thematic groups will be identified and discussed. As the preceding resource assessment has made clear, there is a disparity in the quantity and quality of data available for the various thematic sections, requiring the different topics to respond to different challenges. The agenda items themselves have been generated from discussion amongst the Hadrian's Wall archaeological community and stakeholder groups, and developed in full consultation with them. The scope ranges from the major conceptual issues currently facing mural studies, to specific queries that could be addressed by comparatively low-scale work in the field or archives. It is also important to note that many of the wider agenda items transcend the individual themes. Inevitably further research will both generate new questions and drive re-evaluation of the existing resource. As such it must be stressed that the Agenda is not intended to be prescriptive, it should act as a tool to encourage research, rather than stifling new ways of thinking or avenues of exploration.

1. Cumberland Excavation Committee dug this trench west of Milecastle 48 to search for reducing wing-walls.

In the past, research has focused on elucidating the military history of the frontier zone and as a consequence most resources have been directed towards the Wall and its attendant installations, the forts, and the military bases associated with the Stanegate. Scientific excavations have been conducted for over a century, while antiquarian interest has an even longer pedigree. The heyday of excavation on the Wall was the first-half of the twentieth century, when a succession of key sites were dug and there was a commensurate leap in knowledge. It is also clear, when reading the publications from this period, that bodies such as the Cumberland Excavation Committee were following a research agenda of their own, even if it was never formally committed to paper, and targeting sites that could solve the questions of the day. It is unfair to judge the achievements of these pioneers against modern benchmarks, especially as many of their reports were published to a standard that was ahead of their time, but the quality of the existing data can reasonably be described as variable. This is compounded by the number of excavations undertaken throughout the last century that have yet to be fully published. The potential contribution of further excavation and field survey can hardly be overstated, with recent work on the Wall ditch and the discovery of obstacles on the berm in and around Newcastle demonstrating just how much remains to be learnt about apparently familiar elements.

It is only in more recent times that there has been sustained interest in themes such as pre- and post-Roman usage of the WHS, landscape and environmental studies, the different civilian groups living in the Wall zone and the use of material culture as more than just a dating tool. While the potential of all these areas has been demonstrated, and substantial progress has been made, many avenues of research remain open and further study could revolutionise our understanding of these aspects. It is commonplace amongst many who have not studied Hadrian's Wall in depth that we already know everything that is worth knowing about this frontier system. It is hoped that the following agenda will dispel this notion and demonstrate just how much has still to be learnt about this unique resource.

A.1 The Pre-Roman Archaeology of the Tyne-Solway Isthmus

As this framework is concerned with the Roman-period remains and their immediate context, the Agenda is restricted to Iron Age and, in particular, late pre-Roman Iron Age activity within the region. However, a full understanding of the Iron Age configuration can not be achieved without an appreciation of preceding occupation within the region. Equally, the boundaries of the WHS were not devised to facilitate study of Iron Age activity and much of the key evidence derives from sites outside its limits. Comprehensive prehistoric agendas for the region have already been compiled in the North East and North West Regional Frameworks as well as that for the National Park (Petts 2006; Brennand 2006; Young 2005).

It is reasonable to acknowledge that there has been a historical bias towards the study of the Roman military remains, and the pre-existing dataset for pre-Roman features is correspondingly less extensive. However, building on Jobey's seminal work in the 1950s-1970s, there has been a substantial increase in knowledge of Iron Age activity. Aerial survey is revealing an ever-expanding corpus of sites, surviving as both upstanding monuments and cropmarks, which appear indigenous in style. Yet the absence of the detailed chronological evidence required to assign these features to distinct periods and test the contemporaneity of different elements within individual sites remains a serious limitation. It is unclear how many are pre-Roman, 'Romano-British' or palimpsests of both periods. Environmental evidence has been instrumental in reconstructing Iron Age impact on and management of the landscape, but there is considerable scope for further work, as discussed in the **Landscape and Environment** section of the Agenda. The demonstration of the significance of cord-rig in the 1980s revolutionised understanding of prehistoric agriculture within the North, yet the remains are afflicted by the same chronological limitations as the settlements. In particular, it has been demonstrated that prehistoric-style agriculture was being practised right up until the eve of construction of the frontier at Wallsend, underlining the difficulties involved in divorcing pre-Roman from pre-Hadrianic.

1.1 Locating the resource

1.1.1 It is uncertain how representative the known pre-Roman sites are, in terms of both original density and settlement hierarchy, but it is probable that a considerable proportion await discovery, not least because certain types of site appear to be absent (see below). Gates' aerial survey in 1999 revealed hitherto undetected upstanding indigenous settlements in the intensively studied central sector of the Wall corridor. Even when the sites are identified, interpretation is difficult. While a 'Romano-British' style of indigenous settlement is acknowledged in the Wall zone, there has been little testing of this through excavation and it is unknown whether prehistoric predecessors were standard or exceptional.

1.1.2 The prehistoric infrastructure is almost completely unknown, with the location of tracks and drove-ways entirely uncertain. The local settlement hierarchy is also unclear with, excepting the few hillforts, no evidence for meeting places or central places. Without a wider appreciation of these issues, it is difficult to integrate individual sites into their contemporary context. As well as being of fundamental relevance to establishing contemporary settlement patterns, prehistoric land usage may well have influenced Roman military activity.

1.2 Pre-Roman Iron Age

While beyond the remit of this framework, it is important to acknowledge the need for a more detailed understanding of Neolithic and Bronze Age activity. Just as late Iron Age interaction with the landscape has implications for our understanding of the Roman occupation, so too the development of the landscape must be viewed as a continuum in which the Iron Age inhabitants responded to earlier activity. Key gaps in knowledge are identified and detailed recommendations made in the NWRRF, NERRF and Young (2005).

1.3 Chronology

1.3.1 The chronology for the pre-Roman period remains a serious concern. This is primarily attributable to two factors. Firstly, there is the limited degree of excavation that has been undertaken on pre-Roman features within the WHS. Secondly, even when excavation occurs, the limited use of durable material culture, particularly in the west, and the restricted chronological information this furnishes demands a reliance on absolute scientific dating techniques. However, there are many sites where this has not been attempted. It is clear that structures such as roundhouses were constructed before, throughout and beyond the Roman period, and so accurate dating is critical if individual settlements are to be firmly assigned to a particular period. There is, in general, a pressing need to date a wide range of landscape features.

1.3.2 Although ceramics are scarce in the pre-Roman Iron Age, they are certainly present on sites in the eastern and central sectors. The continuation of these ceramic traditions into the Roman period requires further research, but will be advanced by intensive study of their occurrence (in small but significant quantities) in well-dated contexts on Roman military sites.

1.4 Tribal and geographical boundaries

1.4.1 The Roman historical sources suggest that the north-south boundary between the Votadini and the Brigantian kingdom lay near the Tyne - Solway line. How reliable an indication of the situation on the ground this gives remains debatable, but tribal differences have been invoked for the relative scarcity of hillforts within the Wall corridor. Cultural differences, likely to have been reflected by political boundaries, are evident in the east, on the basis of differences in arable farming between Northumberland and the area south of the Tyne (see below 1.7). The southern farming regimes may coincide with the limits of the

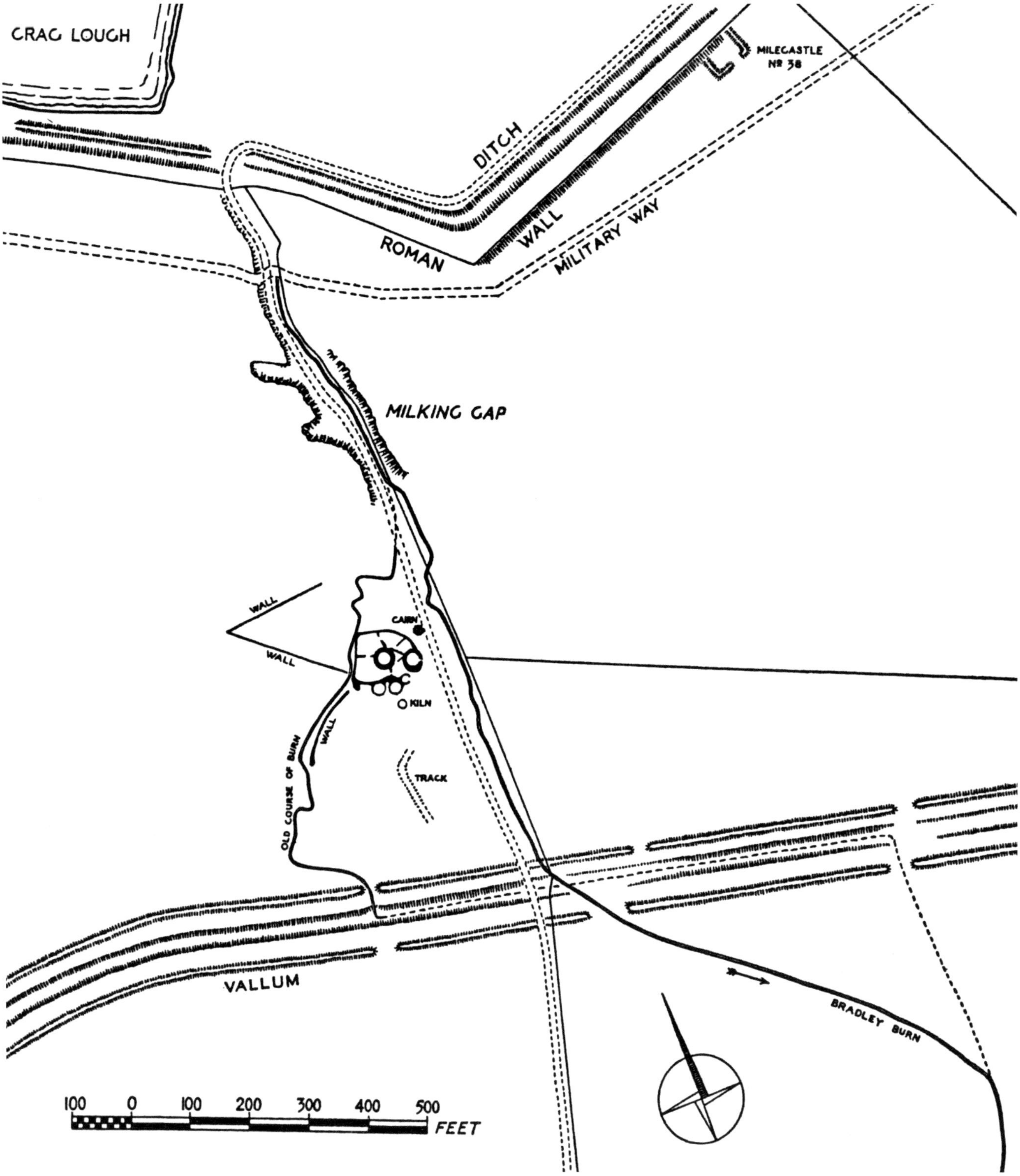

2. Site of the native settlement at Milking Gap in relation to the frontier works

distribution of ceramics, such as butt-beakers, fine wares and amphorae, imported before the Roman conquest. The eastern and central sectors of the Wall lie along the possible borders of these two zones.

1.4.2 The extent to which there was also an east-west divide across the Tyne - Solway corridor is a further consideration. The relative paucity of Iron Age pottery and metalwork west of the Pennines is well known, raising questions about the uniformity of Iron Age activity within the region and the extent to which local economies were integrated.

1.5 Setting settlements within their context

1.5.1 When settlements have been examined, they are often considered individually. There is a need to develop more holistic approaches that recognise such sites as dynamic systems that were integrated into their contemporary context and landscape. This would assist in the generation of a more cohesive picture of Iron Age land management, and serve to complement the existing excavation evidence.

1.5.2 While important progress has been made in reconstructing the prehistoric environment, the existing resource offers great potential for further progress.

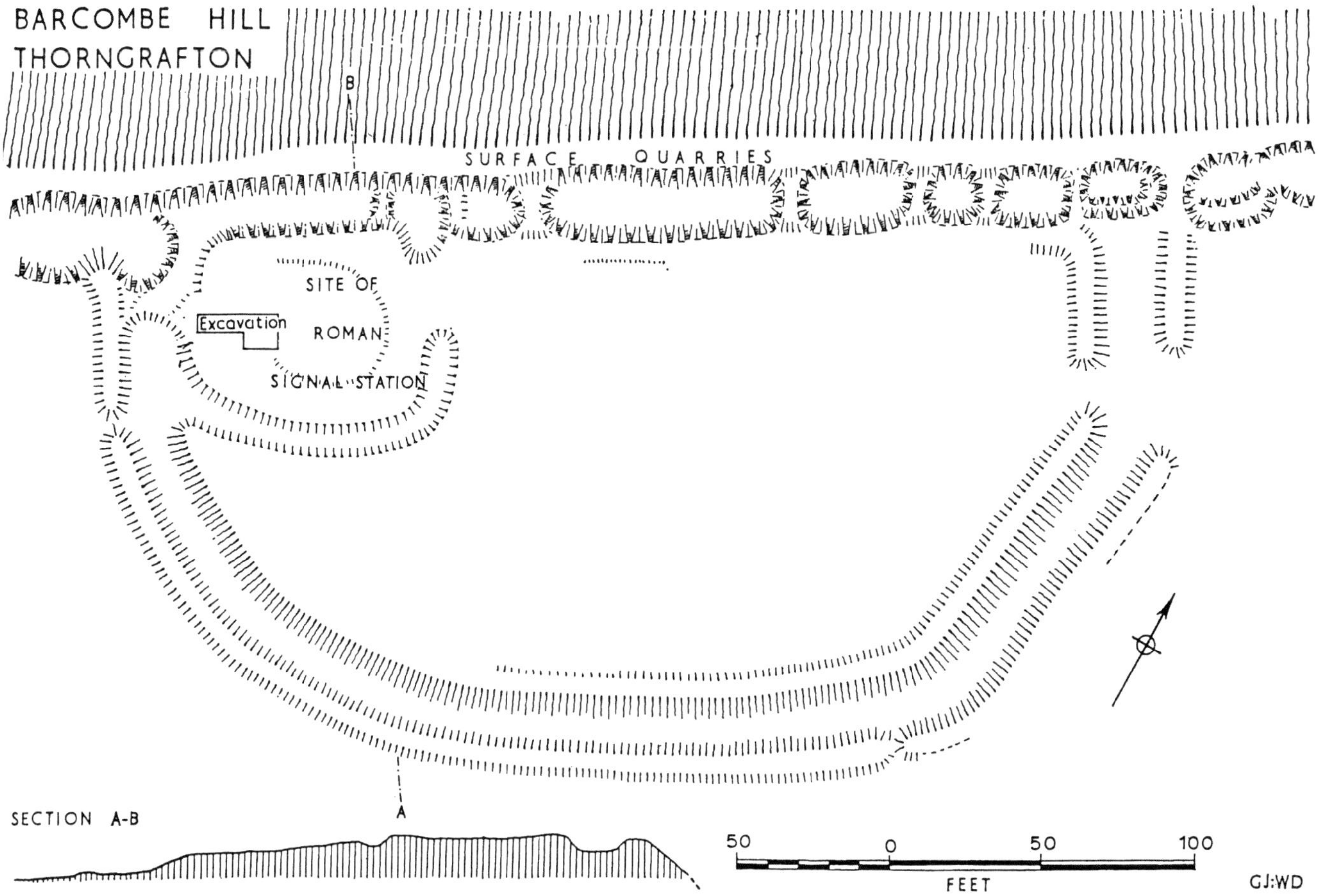

3. The enclosure and Roman installation Barcombe Hill

1.6 Settlement

1.6.1 The sample of Iron Age settlements in the immediate vicinity of the Wall which have been excavated remains small. As such, the corpus of data from the WHS relating to structural elements or the social role of the settlements within the landscape is limited. It is also difficult to demonstrate a link between housing and adjacent plots of cord rig or field systems. Aerial survey continues to yield further examples of probable Iron Age settlements, although without establishing their relative chronologies it remains impossible to estimate even broadly the population density across the region.

1.6.2 While the majority of known prehistoric settlements were enclosed, this may be due to their relative visibility, as open settlements also existed, but these are often only detected by chance. The relative prevalence of these types remains hard to quantify, as do the processes that determined this stylistic difference.

1.6.3 The range of settlement hierarchy along the Tyne-Solway isthmus remains incompletely understood. Hillforts are rare, and there is a shortage of data pertaining to the chronology and usage of those that did exist. Although modest in size, their prominence within the landscape would certainly have ensured local significance. At present their role and date of abandonment, while of considerable importance, remains unclear.

1.7 Economy

1.7.1 The local Iron Age economies remain poorly understood. Van der Veen's (1992) work on crop husbandry regimes has provided some insight into the varying arable economies in the North East, and quernstones are well attested, but beyond this little is known.

1.7.2 More information is required on the specifics of cord rig. There is a need to understand its chronology and formation, as well as the crop grown on it. The technique is known to have been practised right up until the construction of Hadrian's Wall, but after that the picture is unclear. There is, in general, a shortage of data relating to what happened to 'prehistoric' field systems after the Roman conquest. The nature of the relationship between or dependency of the tribal elite upon agriculture is entirely unclear.

1.7.3 The limited material culture preserves few indications of cottage industries or social stratification, but the very nature of the evidence makes broad generalisations difficult. Metal objects from the area are scarce, as is the evidence for their production and working. Most of the direct evidence that is available for Iron Age economies other than agriculture comes from outside the WHS and the NWRRF and NERRF should be consulted for the wider regional context.

1.8 Religion and burial

1.8.1 Iron Age burials are almost unknown within the region, and this may well be attributable to the adoption of mortuary practises that have left little mark on the archaeological record, such as excarnation and urnless cremation. However, the presence of an inhumation cut by a tower on the Cumberland Coast and the crouched inhumations from Cumbria suggest that more visible funerary rites could occur. Without absolute dating there is a danger that Iron Age burials will be assigned to other periods.

1.8.2 As elsewhere in England during this period, religious practises remain obscure. Most information about the names and nature of local deities derives from Roman-period inscriptions, dedications and depictions. However, even those gods and goddesses with Celtic names could have been imported by the auxiliary units and so the extent to which they can inform our view of pre-Roman religion is entirely unclear. It is certain that even if indigenous, the evidence relates to a period when they were being worshipped through a filter of *Romanitas* and so cannot give a reliable indication of earlier rites. Votive offerings and bog bodies may provide a starting point, but there is currently insufficient material capable of synthesis.

1.9 Pre-Roman/Roman interface

1.9.1 The Wall zone offers considerable potential for further study of the interface between the Iron Age and Roman periods. While the physical impact of Rome in the form of forts and roads is clear, the effect of this on the indigenous population is not. Questions ranging from the extent of local elite interaction with the occupiers, to resistance to Roman rule, challenge existing methodologies. More traditional approaches such as establishing continuity or abandonment of settlement in the immediate vicinity of the frontier also have implications for our perceptions of this critical period. There is a need to understand the relationship between indigenous settlements and Roman forts or urban areas. Where native settlements are situated close to the Wall, it is particularly important to determine their chronology. Did they, for example, originate in the pre-Roman period and, if so, was occupation ended by intervention of the Roman military when the Hadrianic frontier came into being? Alternatively, did occupation continue into, or even beyond, the Roman period?

1.9.2 The extent to which the arrival of the Roman army can be linked to an increasingly intensive exploitation of the landscape remains disputed (see 5.7.8). The relative impact of the Iron Age population and Roman army on timber stocks may help to explain variations in the use of material within the frontier zone.

1.9.3 The boundaries of the WHS were not designed for the study of the Wall in its wider context and it is important to acknowledge that Iron Age tribal groups which existed outside of this area, such as those to the north, could have had a significant impact on the development of the frontier zone. The accumulation of further data pertaining to such tribes remains essential.

A.2 The Pre-Hadrianic Frontier on the Tyne - Solway Isthmus, and The Stanegate

This theme covers a range of elements associated with the Roman occupation of the isthmus, spanning the earliest datable military activity in the Tyne-Solway corridor, at Carlisle, and some of the latest, at sites such as Vindolanda and Newbrough. The term 'Stanegate' is being used in its broadest sense here to refer to a series of sites that lay to the south of Hadrian's Wall and either pre-date the Hadrianic frontier or were contemporary with it. The term itself derives from the medieval name for the road that can be traced, at least in part, between Carlisle and Corbridge. Since then it has been used as a wider descriptive term referring to both the military installations along the road, and, more controversially, to a number that lie to the east and west of its known course. Scientific excavations have been conducted throughout the twentieth century and continue, with the long-running research excavations at South Shields and Vindolanda, up to the present day. The Stanegate resource then, compels us to address a range of challenges, including a dependence on data of varying quality, major theories based on incompletely published excavations and the recurrent question of what it is that constitutes a frontier.

2.1 Locating the resource

2.1.1 Despite huge leaps forward at Carlisle and Vindolanda, our knowledge of Flavian dispositions on the Isthmus is undoubtedly far from complete, owing to the lack of archaeological visibility of sometimes short-lived early sites. Conversely the continuing excavations at Vindolanda have revealed just how complex a sequence of forts can precede visible sites and it remains likely that early forts elsewhere have been obscured by their successors, as, for example, at Carvoran. In addition we are wholly ignorant of the extent of any first-century occupation at points on the east and west coasts, with our mental map of the Flavian Isthmus still dominated by the patterns of occupation along the advance roads north via Corbridge and Carlisle.

2.1.2 Ascertaining the course of the Stanegate road, as well as any extension of it beyond Corbridge and Carlisle, remains a fundamental requirement. Now that we have abandoned the idea that installations were regularly spaced on the pre-Hadrianic isthmus, the number of 'missing' sites cannot be reliably estimated, either for the section between Carlisle and Corbridge, or for the sectors further east and west. There is currently a divergence in installation density between the east and west, although it is uncertain whether this is real or apparent. The extant incidence of only isolated examples of watchtowers is a further contrast with pre-Hadrianic frontiers on the Continent, but it may simply be that more towers await discovery.

2.1.3 The western and eastern Stanegate 'extensions' remain putative, but are of crucial relevance to perceptions of both the purpose of the forces on the Stanegate proper, and the build-up to the mural frontier. There is a need to follow up recent work by the Hadrian's Wall NMP at the

4. Site of the fort at Carlisle

western end and definitively test the character of linear features and other sites there that have been claimed as pre-Hadrianic frontier works, although this may only be possible via extensive programmes of excavation utilising scientific dating. If not Roman in origin, such features will very probably be of pre-Roman or Roman Iron Age date, and their investigation would be of importance in its own right in characterising the indigenous society of the western Wall-zone.

2.2 Chronology

Outside the major closely dated sequences at Corbridge, Vindolanda and Carlisle, the date and chronological development of other elements of the pre-Hadrianic isthmus are very poorly understood. There is a pressing need for dating evidence from sites such as Washingwells, in order to establish how the installations to the east and west of the Stanegate slot in to the overall chronology. Controversy surrounds the dating of a number of sites which have been excavated, with Haltwhistle Burn, for instance, being assigned variously Trajanic and Hadrianic origins. Precise dating of such smaller structures is urgently required to resolve the issue of the existence of a frontier on the Stanegate. Furthermore the recent suggestion that the Stanegate road postdates the establishment of the military bases along the Tyne-Solway corridor focuses attention on the chronological relationship between these elements.

2.3 Existing data

2.3.1 There is a poverty of information regarding most of the Stanegate sites, few of which have enjoyed area-excavation using modern techniques. There are no extensive untapped archives to supplement the well-known publications of pioneering excavations at sites such as Old Church, Brampton and Haltwhistle Burn. Only future excavation may be capable of resolving uncertainties, especially at the latter, the only Stanegate fortlet known to be well-preserved. It would also be appropriate to re-evaluate the results of research on the "Western Stanegate" beyond Carlisle. Determining the sequence of development at sites such as Burgh-by-Sands could have far-reaching implications for our understanding of the build up to a frontier in this region.

2.3.2 The existing data should be set within the landscape and topographic context. It would also be appropriate to clarify the relationship between the Stanegate installations and pre-existing settlement patterns. In this connection we still lack solid information about the nature of 'first contact' with the indigenous poplulation during the Flavian conquest of the area. Despite the ever tighter chronology of foundation date achieved at sites such as Carlisle and Vindolanda, the impact of the arrival of the Roman army remains to be documented in the archaeology of any contemporary native settlement. Under the Wall-forts, on the other hand, there is evidence that the local tradition of Iron Age agriculture was carried out without interruption

5. Aqueduct fed fountain at Corbridge

until disrupted by the building of the Wall. On the whole, the potential for Roman military sites to seal and preserve the last stage of preceding Iron Age activity has not been fully appreciated or exploited.

2.3.3 It is hard to overstate the importance of the insight into day-to-day activity at Vindolanda during the late first and early second centuries that the writing-tablets have afforded. Future discoveries will undoubtedly provide further details and may provide insights into contemporary perceptions of the role of this zone in the period before AD 120.

2.3.4 Geophysical survey has recently revolutionised our knowledge of the Wall-forts and the military *vici*, but has not been applied extensively to the pre-Hadrianic sites (except for Carvoran, and Castlesteads, sometimes taken to be a pre-Hadrianic fort). Here it would have an obvious role in elucidating sites so poorly known through modern excavation plans.

2.4 The Stanegate frontier

Debate about the possible existence and nature of a Trajanic frontier on the Stanegate has been ongoing for over 70 years. Although many of the sites proposed by Birley in his scheme of regularly spaced installations have not been located, a lack of regularity need not prejudice our judgement of the Stanegate sites as a pre-Hadrianic frontier cordon. A clear understanding of Trajanic intentions for the Tyne-Solway corridor would enable us to set Hadrian's Wall within its immediate military context. Such understanding is only likely to be gained as a result of more accurate dating of installations to ascertain by how much they pre-date the Wall. It is also vital for this understanding to obtain a closer knowledge of the date and circumstances of the abandonment of sites north of the Isthmus, and the date and function of military sites on the Devil's Causeway.

2.5 The Stanegate and Hadrian's Wall

Much remains to be understood about the continuation of the Stanegate as the main east-west communications corridor for the Wall. Although it is reasonably certain it had this role, we know little in detail about branch routes that linked the Wall and its forts to this main route. The possibility that a Hadrianic road (pre-dating the Military Way) was supplied to serve those parts of the Wall distant from the Stanegate (and that in places, such as Irthington, this road has been mistaken for the Stanegate) still requires investigation. Finally, the role and character of those Stanegate forts that survived in use after the garrisoning of the Wall is not well-understood: excavated parts of the fort at Carlisle were turned over to industrial use in the Hadrianic period, but it is not known how typical this is of the fort as a whole, or whether this occurred at other Stanegate sites that continued in occupation.

2.6 Urban centres

In the later Roman period the Stanegate served as a main road linking the two greatest urban centres of the northern frontier. The development of urbanism within the Wall-zone is an area where further research is desirable. Whether Corbridge should be regarded as a *caput civitatis* remains unclear, although there is evidence that Carlisle can be linked with the *civitas Carvetiorum*. These sites represent the densest concentrations of civilians within the Wall-zone. We do not understand the reasons why they flourished in the wake of the decline or disapperarance of the fort *vici* by the early-fourth century. Their growth as civil centres coincides with the cessation of epigraphic commemoration and therefore hardly anything is known of their social make-up or economic basis in the fourth century. While they would have served as central places within their hinterland, little is known of their immediate landscape setting, or of the character of "indigenous" settlement in their hinterland in the late-Roman period, although in this connection the potential of the site at Hawkhirst, 2.5km south of the Wall at Brampton, should be noted.

A.3 The Wall

One of the great strengths of the Wall resource, the huge quantity of data available, is also one of its greatest challenges. A considerable proportion of the accessible Wall installations have been subject to varying degrees of excavation, although this attention has not been divided equally. There has been a concentration on the turrets and milecastles at the expense of the Vallum, Wall ditch and temporary camps. It is also only comparatively recently that the Wall itself has been treated with the same degree of care as its attendant structures and excavated rather than disinterred. Many of the earlier excavations were interpreted through the then current framework of Wall periods, and it would be timely to re-evaluate them in the light of more recent research. Progress is also hampered by a number of important unpublished excavations. More positively, development-driven archaeology has revealed how well-preserved archaeological deposits can survive in urban contexts, while new discoveries continue to demand re-evaluation of apparently familiar frontier elements. Consensus concerning the fundamental question of the function of the Wall remains as elusive as ever.

6. The Wall on Walltown Crags

3.1 Locating the resource

A central concern is that there are stretches where the precise course and distribution of the frontier installations and infrastructure remain uncertain. The eastern and western termini of the Vallum and western terminus of the Wall remain unknown, and it has recently been questioned whether the Wall did cross the marshes in Wall-miles 73 - 76 (Biggins et al 2004). Although the general course of much of the Wall under modern Newcastle and Wallsend is established, the sequence of milecastles and turrets east of Denton requires clarification, so that the full implications of the dislocated Westgate Road milecastle can be understood. Away from the central sector, the line of the military way is frequently obscure. Details of many specific elements remain desirable, including what provisions were made for the road crossing west of Stanwix and the location and form of the bridge over the Tyne at Newcastle.

3.2 Existing data

3.2.1 The key challenges associated with managing and utilising the existing data come in two forms. Firstly there is the continued reliance on the results of research conducted when both the knowledge of the Wall and the development of appropriate archaeological techniques were in their infancy. While the sheer quantity of data available is one of the great strengths of the resource, there is a need to revisit old excavations, so that earlier conclusions can be re-evaluated in the light of current knowledge. Very few archives relating to published excavations on the line of the Wall which are capable of yielding useful new information survive, and consequently significant new detail is most likely to be obtained through new excavations.

7. The course of the Wall under Westgate Road, Newcastle

3.2.2 The publication backlog must be addressed. The unpublished material from the Wall zone represents an extremely important research resource, which considerable amounts of time and money have been devoted to acquiring, and the analysis and dissemination of this material needs to be regarded as an extremely high priority. Conclusions cannot be drawn from data which cannot be interrogated, hindering an informed interpretation of these sites.

3.2.3 There is a considerable divergence in the quantity of available data between the western sector and the central and eastern sectors. This is primarily attributable to the history of research in the region, which often targeted the better preserved structures in the central and eastern sectors. While important work in more recent decades has begun to address this imbalance, further data from the western end which establishes the position of all the installations and elucidates the structural and chronological development of the frontier is essential.

3.3 Chronology

3.3.1 Establishing the chronological relationship between the key Wall elements was a major research priority in the first half of the twentieth century. While considerable progress was made, major gaps in knowledge still remain. The dating of many of the changes and adaptations to the Wall and its associated structures remains imprecise, while some relationships have become more complicated in the face of new discoveries. The rebuilding of the western end of the Turf Wall in stone and the commissioning of the extra Narrow Wall are, in particular, key developments whose interpretation is hindered by the absence of closer dating.

Very little is known about the maintenance of the Wall in the later third and fourth centuries (i.e. for rather more than half its lifetime in the Roman period).

3.3.2 The potential for dendrochronological analysis has been neglected. The area around Burgh is suitable for this, given the references to Wall remains supported on wooden piles in antiquarian reports.

3.3.3 It is almost forty years since the Hadrianic building programme has been considered in the light of its very rich collection of associated epigraphic material.

3.4 Materials

While the principal materials utilised during construction and repair of the frontier are known, their precise source is often only broadly attested. With the exception of those cases where Roman graffiti or hoards have been found, and obviously modern workings, few of the quarries in the WHS have been dated. The source of the lime used in the mortar is also uncertain. The reason why the original Hadrianic superstructure was divided into stone and turf stretches remains uncertain.

3.5 Structures

3.5.1 Function
The precise manner in which the Wall structures interacted and the resulting frontier system functioned remains a source of considerable debate. It is also unclear whether alterations to the frontier over time were refinements to the original scheme or indicate shifts in approach and possibly also function. Alongside this are concerns that our perception has been filtered by a concept of the Wall as a single entity. There is a need to look at variation along the course of the Wall - such as the elimination of the turrets and apparent decline in importance of the central sector. It would, in general, be appropriate to test a range of accepted facts to ensure that we have a reliable picture of the basic frontier elements.

3.5.2 The curtain
There are some very basic needs that can be usefully addressed, such as establishing the width of the Wall, foundations and footings at a succession of sites along the frontier. At present there is a bias in such data towards the central and, to a lesser extent, eastern sectors. The nature of the upper rampart furniture, including any wall-walk, remains controversial, but could potentially be resolved if an area of *in situ* collapse were detected.

3.5.3 The ditch
Recent research on the ditch has begun to redress an historical imbalance that saw only limited work undertaken on it. However, there is still a shortage of full ditch profiles and a lack of detailed dimensions, particularly when including the counterscarp and glacis. The implications of the failure to complete the ditch at points where the bedrock made cutting it too arduous, such as Allolee Rigg and Limestone Corner, particularly when the Vallum ploughs through the latter, remain obscure. There are a number of problems (some of which have only very recently become apparent) concerning the relationship of the Ditch to other structures: the arrangement of the Wall-ditch at forts, the presence or absence of causeways at milecastle gates, the possible presence of obstacles beyond the ditch, the narrowing of the berm at turrets, and the possible re-digging of the ditch and restoration of standard berm widths at turrets following their demolition.

8. The Wall Ditch terminates as the curtain rises up on to Sewingshields

3.5.4 Obstacles
The presence of obstacles on the berm is now well established in Wallsend and Newcastle and as far west as Throckley, but much remains to be learnt about their wider distribution. Recent discoveries suggest that that they were renewed in some places on at least two occasions, so there are important questions of chronology to be resolved.

9. Milecastle 42

3.5.5 Milecastles
Alongside more intangible questions, such as who could pass through their gates, a range of directly addressable issues exist. Although there is considerable evidence for activities occurring outside the milecastle walls, extramural features have only rarely been sought, hindering an appreciation of the milecastles' immediate context. It remains uncertain whether Stone Wall milecastles were originally equipped with stone or timber barracks and whether there were towers over both gates. The source of their garrisons and the duration of their tour of duty are also contentious. The narrowing of the milecastle gates and apparent elimination of the ditch causeways is of fundamental relevance to our interpretation of the frontier, but only imprecisely dated. Evidence for the nature of third- and fourth-century internal buildings is strictly limited, although finds would support continued occupation at many sites.

10. Turret 29a

3.5.6 Turrets

While fundamental to any conception of their role, reconstructions of the height and finish of these structures remain hard to test. Excavation has also concentrated on their interior rather than their immediate surroundings. The mechanism by which turrets were later eliminated or retained is not fully understood. New perspectives on the dating of second-century coarse pottery will require a reassessment of the turret finds.

3.5.7 The Vallum

Much remains uncertain about this unique feature, including its original purpose. More specific queries include whether there were originally causeways at the milecastles, the origins of the marginal mound and its relationship to both the original specifications for the earthwork and the later crossings. The purpose of intermittent stretches of metalling on the north, and occasionally south, Vallum berm is unclear, as is the process of silting and filling of the ditch. There is no definitive answer to questions pertaining to the dating and implications of the slighting, filling and, possibly, reconditioning of the earthwork.

3.5.8 Camps

The temporary camps within the Tyne-Solway corridor represent a significant proportion of those known in England, but have received only intermittent attention. In particular their purpose(s) and chronology remain entirely uncertain, while there has been only occasional and restricted investigation of their interiors. Careful exploration of this latter has potential to reveal indications of the size and type of unit, as well as the length of stay or degree of later reuse. The success of C14 dating for the camp at Kintore in Scotland indicates the potential of this resource. More detailed information is a prerequisite to understanding the activities and intentions of the units that built these camps.

3.5.9 Bridges

The stone bridges of Hadrian's Wall, together with those on Dere Street, collectively represent perhaps the best examples of this building-type in the North-Western provinces. Their remains are vulnerable to instantaneous and unpredicatable flood events, which are becoming far more common as river regimes change. They might also be affected by flood-protection schemes, together with other riverine features such as Roman water-mills. Research and conservation policies are urgently required to deal with these threats. Almost nothing is known about culverts through the Wall at the points were it crossed smaller burns and waterways.

11. The site of the North Tyne bridge, with monumental masonry visible in the channel

3.6 The Western Extension

A number of fundamental aspects relating to the cordon of sites running around the Cardurnock peninsula and down the Cumberland Coast require re-evaluation to clarify their interpretation. In particular, the status of the possible linear barrier provided in conjunction with the coastal installations around the Cardurnock Peninsula must be addressed. A considerable number of installations have yet to be located, and the southerly terminus of the system is uncertain. Questions remain about the evolution of both the coastal towers and the system as a whole. Whether or not the extant coastal defences were the product of a single plan or developed in stages needs to be investigated. While many milefortlet sites have been detected, the limited nature of the trenching in the majority of cases prevents a detailed evaluation of their internal layout. The road servicing the coastal installations represents an essential part of the system, but its course is almost entirely unknown. How much of the system was brought back into commission following the return from the Antonine Wall, and for how long, remains debatable, as does the nature of any fourth-century reuse.

A.4 The Forts and Extramural Settlement

Second only to the substantial settlements at Corbridge and Carlisle, the greatest population density in the Wall zone occurred at the forts. In addition to the auxiliary units were the extramural settlements or military *vici* that grew up outside the forts. Geophysical survey has recently demonstrated the extent of these extramural developments, yet despite a few notable exceptions previous research has primarily concentrated on the forts themselves. Some of these excavations remain unpublished, although important progress in clearing the backlog has been made. A third element is the cemeteries which were established outside the forts and remain, for the most part, untapped resources. Many of the agenda items focus on the need for a greater understanding of the interrelationship between forts and their extramural settlement.

4.1 Chronology

Although the general place of the Wall forts within the building order of the frontier is now established, much remains to be learnt about the chronology of the coastal and inland forts at the western end of the Wall and along the Cumberland Coast. Whether those on the latter had Trajanic predecessors or were the product of a Wall-style fort decision is still uncertain. Further research is also required on how long the Wall forts were occupied for and the degree to which periods of abandonment can be detected. In particular, more data are needed to clarify the date at which the outpost forts were abandoned. The development of fort internal plans needs to be better understood. The extent to which structural alterations or destruction deposits within a group of forts can be linked to give a wider insight into events on the frontier remains contentious.

4.2 Structure

4.2.1 While considerable work was undertaken on the structural elements of the forts during the twentieth century, further avenues of research exist. The overall Hadrianic fort plan is only reasonably clear at Wallsend, and it is uncertain to what extent the later plans at other forts reflect the original configuration.

4.2.2 It would be appropriate to evaluate critically how secure the interpretation of a range of fort buildings is: doubts surround the identification and function of buildings interpreted as hospitals, workshops and store-houses. Rampart-back buildings have scarcely been examined and their possible functions include barracks, stables, workshops and cook-houses. Determining the purpose of the circular structures at Vindolanda remains highly desirable.

4.2.3 Concern remains about the extent to which the excavated building types offer a representative sample. Infantry barrack blocks are prominent amongst the structural types that it would be desirable to subject to further examination, particularly if examples which are likely to contain surviving floor levels could be targeted. Cavalry barracks have now been securely identified, but their development in the third and fourth centuries is only partly understood.

12. The stone barrack blocks at Chesters

13. Triple ditch system under excavation at Birdoswald

4.2.4 How far does the archaeological evidence reflect that from epigraphy? Can the latter provide the basis for an intervention on the ground? It could, for instance, be instructive to see whether the sequence of events recorded at the Birdoswald commander's house, for instance, tallies with the archaeological evidence.

4.2.5 The tactical significance, or otherwise, of multiple ditches at some forts remains a source of debate, while the ditches themselves constitute a neglected resource in terms of the paleo-environmental evidence they contain.

14. Superstructure of the *principia* strongroom, Chesters

4.2.6 Excavations have altered our perceptions of change in forts during the third and fourth centuries, but much remains uncertain: major topics include the arrangement and development of barrack accommodation, the question of how irregular units were accommodated, the ritual and ceremonial use of streets in forts, particularly in relation to changes in the importance of the *principia*, different use of granaries and in the arrangements for the distribution of supplies and preparation of food stuffs (including the presence of fourth-century markets in forts), and variations in fort buildings which might be connected with the abandonment of extra-mural buildings, such as the construction of internal baths.

4.2.7 The Hadrian's Wall forts represent an extraordinarily well-preserved sample but they need to be studied as part of the overall *corpus* of Roman military fortifications drawn from all the provinces of the empire. An assessment of their international importance is needed, but it would probably be not too far wide of the mark to suggest that their particular contribution - where they fill the largest gap in our overall knowledge - is from the late second to early fourth centuries.

4.2.8 Architecture is often a neglected field, but ideas about the appearance of buildings have changed dramatically over the last 40 years. The level of preservation of internal buildings, defensive structures and extramural settlement makes the forts in the WHS uniquely suited to testing models for the reconstruction of original building styles.

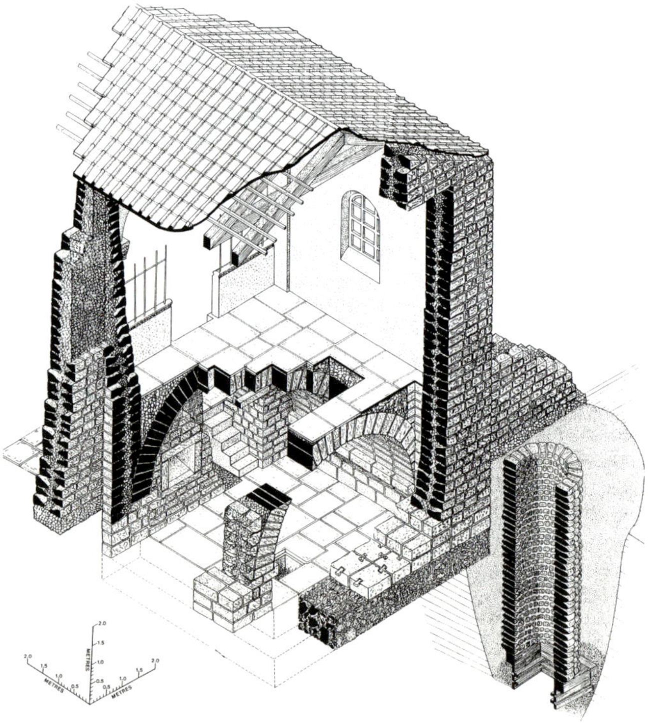

15. Reconstruction drawing of *principia* strongroom

4.3 Garrisons

4.3.1 Direct evidence relating to which units were in occupation and over what timescale is partial at best for many sites. It would be appropriate to review the evidence for when unit sizes change and how this relates to variations in barrack accommodation. Determining the ethnic composition of a garrison remains a priority, and study of cemeteries, diet, food supply and pottery all hold potential for this. However, known burial areas appear too

16. Strip building in the military *vicus* at Vindolanda

small for the postulated population over a 300-year period and more information is needed on where cemeteries are and how extensive they were. Were burial grounds 'single period' sites continuing for 300 years or multiple sites with discrete chronologies?

4.3.2 Fort refuse dumps would also be a valuable resource if they could be located, and may provide data for ethnicity, as well as food preparation within the forts, which, beyond the existence of ovens in the *intervallum*, remains ittle understood.

4.3.3 The presence of women, slaves and other civilians within forts remains a contentious issue. As does the overall social composition and the varying use of material culture by *milites*, centurions and commanding officers.

4.3.4 Little is known about cultural assimilation in the frontier zone and the balance between classical, provincial and local ideals and expressions of identity over time.

4.4 Location

4.4.1 It is important to gain a broader understanding of the factors that determined the siting of the outpost forts. The suggestion that the forts were positioned in areas where there was less intensive indigenous settlement require testing. This need is heightened by proposals that the wider fort distribution was influenced by the density of pre-existing settlement and the nature of indigenous politics.

4.4.2 While it is unlikely that any forts remain undetected on the line of the Wall itself, it is entirely possible that further installations of this type existed within the frontier zone.

4.5 Infrastructure

4.5.1 There is a general need to understand forts within their landscape context. More specifically, the network of roads supporting the forts requires detailed attention. The extent of the individual forts' *territoria* is entirely unclear.

4.5.2 Where appropriate riverine and coastal facilities, including wharves and jetties, may be directly relevant to our perception of the role of the associated fort. However, in many cases they have not been systematically sought, and in others, such as the South Shields harbour, they continue to defy detection. Determining the existence and scale of such works remains highly desirable. It is also possible that remains of Roman-period wrecks may survive in the tidal reaches of rivers and on the east and west coasts.

4.5.3 Knowledge of water management systems within the forts would benefit from further research. While there is evidence of pressurised pipes, water junctions and gravity feed from Carlisle, the mechanisms of water supply at many of the forts remain uncertain. Fort drainage systems are also only partially known, but represent a potential source of paleo-environmental evidence.

Extramural Settlements

The restricted investigation of extramural settlements on Hadrian's Wall is a limitation when it comes to assessing the development and range of services available within these extramural settlements, as well as their wider economic role. There are a series of outstanding questions relating to the relationship between them and their associated forts.

4.6 Chronology

4.6.1 Many chronological aspects pertaining to extramural settlement remain only imprecisely understood. There is evidence for second-century extramural settlements at Birdoswald, Housesteads, Rudchester, Wallsend and South Shields, but it is still unclear how soon after the establishment of a fort they would typically be founded. While geophysical survey has recently demonstrated the size of those extramural settlements directly adjacent to the forts, the earliest extramural settlement buildings at Housesteads appear to have developed to the south of the Vallum. This discovery is potentially of considerable importance in determining the origins of the extramural settlements, but it is still unclear whether this practice is paralleled elsewhere.

4.6.2 The end of the extramural settlements also requires further clarification. Current evidence indicates that many were abandoned in the mid/late third century and it remains necessary to determine whether there was any continuation after this date. This can be linked to the wider need to identify those factors, economic, military or social, which precipitated abandonment or ensured survival.

4.7 Structures and layout

4.7.1 While a variety of building types are known to have existed in the extramural settlements, their full range has yet to be determined. Given the evidence for some degree of self-regulation within these communities, including reference to magistrates, it may be possible to identify basic civic buildings, such as a meeting-house. It is conceivable that further official buildings, in addition to the *mansiones*, existed. Although the presence of temples and shrines is well attested further work on such structures remains desirable. In particular there is the question of the extent to which such structures represent a fusion between classical models and local traditions, at a provincial and inter-provincial level, and the implications of this.

4.7.2 Geophysical survey has made an enormous contribution to our understanding of the extramural settlements and retains the potential to provide further insights into the nature and extent of these settlements. While the plans themselves cannot furnish chronological data, the opportunities they provide for the precise targeting of key structures should be followed up.

4.7.3 It is unclear whether there was any formal layout to the extramural settlements and the existence of zoning by function or class within them remains a possibility. In particular it would be worth investigating whether different social classes, including servile elements, can be identified in extramural settlements from the varying types and standards of buildings or finds.

4.7.4 The discovery, by geophysical survey, of buildings north of the Wall at Birdoswald, the excavation of a timber building beyond the east gate at Wallsend and the earlier references to buildings north of Chesters, are of fundamental relevance to perceptions of the role of the frontier. As well as the need to clarify how common an occurrence this was, and at what period, it raises questions relating to whether there were differences - ethnic or social - between the inhabitants of this area of extramural settlement and those dwelling south of the Wall.

4.7.5 The degree to which the individual extramural settlements were shaped by their wider context is uncertain. Were character and function dictated primarily by the nature of the fort with which an extramural settlement was associated, or did the topographical setting, proximity to major watercourses or nature of the surrounding indigenous population also play a significant role? The degree to which the character and function of the extramural settlements varied from site to site cannot yet be quantified.

4.8 Inhabitants

Attempts to achieve a wider understanding of the extramural settlements are hindered by a shortage of information pertaining to who lived, worked in or used the extramural settlements. Most fundamentally there is a need to clarify the origins and identities of the *vicani,* as well as what happened to them when the extramural settlements were abandoned. Differences in material culture between the forts and the extramural settlements may provide a more detailed insight into the relationship and activities of the inhabitants of these two entities.

4.9 Economy

The economic character of the extramural settlements is inextricably linked to many of the preceding agenda points but remains imprecisely understood. Interdisciplinary study of the existing material, in conjunction with fresh excavation is required to advance understanding of this fundamental aspect.

A.5 Landscape and Environment

This theme is of fundamental relevance to our understanding of every period of human activity within the Tyne-Solway corridor. Indeed, in terms of the landscape, it is important not to restrict ourselves to the narrow cordon of the WHS, but seek to set the monument within its wider context. A co-ordinated view of the Wall within its landscape would help to offset the bias in the data set towards individual sites. There is also a pressing need to date those landscape elements that are known to us. The potential of pollen studies to provide important information on the development and management of the prehistoric and Roman landscape has already been demonstrated and it would be beneficial to develop a sampling strategy. The build-up of silt and sediment within the Wall ditch and Vallum remains a largely untapped resource. The topical theme of climate fluctuation has an important contemporary resonance, with interpretations of the conditions on Hadrian's Wall being deployed in popular media by both sides of the global-warming debate.

Some of the agenda items below refer to specific and tightly focused questions to ask of the landscape and environment but the majority are much broader and attempt to integrate with more traditional studies for understanding the Wall. The Wall was built in an existing dynamic landscape which continued to evolve, through both natural and human causes and effects, as it does even today.

Given the huge range of interests on the Wall, the equally huge range of existing datasets (many spatial) and the modern availability of powerful computers it is a serious limitation that a Hadrian's Wall GIS has yet to be established. This would provide an essential tool to assist effective synthesis and understanding, and should also greatly help implementation of best management strategies. The GIS would also assist narrative linking the different classes of material, so that we can attempt the wider analyses that the significance of the landscape demands.

5.1 Scope

5.1.1 The WHS has strictly defined boundaries but these are not designed for studying the Wall in its wider landscape. There is the need to attempt to determine the extent of the Wall's hinterland to the south as well as the zone of exploitation to the north.

5.1.2 The scope needs to be multi-period since the Wall was built and used in a dynamic landscape.

5.1.3 There should be greater effort made to draw in analogies from studies of the landscapes and environments of other frontiers, especially perhaps those in the wider, international WHS.

5.1.4 The scope of even the major Roman sites along the Wall frontier is required. This is especially the case in relation to the juxtaposition of fort and associated settlements and how they fitted into their surroundings. Some were clearly put in defensive positions on high ground with others guarding routeways and river crossings. Others, such as Stanwix, were located on unfavourable waterlogged sites even though apparently drier ground was available not that far away.

17. Excavating Beckfoot cemetery threatened by coastal erosion

5.1.5 Scope is also relevant to archaeological resource management: several sites are actively eroding especially into the sea or rivers. Ravenglass fort and Beckfoot cemetery, for instance, are both suffering from coastal erosion; this will continue and will ultimately lead to the loss of the resource. By understanding the dynamics of the erosion it might be possible to erect sustainable defences or to target excavation of the most vulnerable areas. Such choices will almost certainly be needed for sites in actively erosive environments under current unstable climatic regimes.

5.1.6 Much of the work to-date has been a detailed look at specific sites rather than a co-ordinated view of the Wall and its landscape. There needs to be better integration of the different classes of material and wider application of environmental science techniques to archaeological investigations. There needs to be better synthesis of these data but a consideration of who, and fundamentally how, this work can proceed also is required.

5.2 Chronology

5.2.1 Chronologies of the structural elements of the Wall are reasonably well understood even if not precise enough for some questions to be addressed. However the broader chronology of the landscape is not and there is a need for dating the landscape stratigraphies revealed by aerial and earthwork survey, especially where, for instance, land boundaries can be related to settlements.

5.2.2 We need to know more about the native economy locally and particularly about the capacity of native farmers to generate surpluses of food or livestock for sale or the payment of taxes. One major problem here, as in Northumberland generally, is the poor preservation of bone on most settlement sites.

5.2.3 As well as relations between Roman and native, there

Table 1 Chart showing where environmental work has been undertaken along the line of the Wall

Wall sites with environmental work

qualitative score for amount of work done to analytical phase

							NOT COMPLETE	
	excav'n	bone	seeds	invertebrates	pollen	soils	geophysics	notes
South Shields	extensive	moderate	extensive					large numbers to assess
Wallsend	extensive	moderate	few		little			poor preservation
Newcastle	moderate	moderate	moderate					
Bottle Bank, Gateshead	moderate	??	moderate					
Washingwells, Whickham							yes, not clear Roman	
Benwell	extensive							
Rudchester	moderate							
Halton Chesters	extensive						part of fort and vicus	
Corbridge	extensive	extensive						interpretation limited as at site level only
Chesters	extensive	few	few					
Carrawburgh	moderate							
Houseteads	extensive	moderate	moderate					
Vindolanda	extensive	extensive	moderate				vicus parts	bones currently being analysed
Peel Gap	moderate		few					
Haltwhistle Burn	minimal							
Great Chesters	some							
Carvoran	some		few				vicus	
Throp	minimal							
Birdoswald	extensive	extensive	extensive		little		vicus	
Nether Denton	some							turf rampart, cremation
Castlesteads	minimal							
Old Church, Brampton	minimal							turf rampart
Stanwix	extensive	few	few	few	little	moderate		
Carlisle	extensive	extensive	extensive	extensive	little	minimal		
Burgh by Sands	minimal							
Drumburgh	some							
Kirkbride	some	few						timber structures
Bowness	moderate							
Beckfoot	moderate	human	charcoal					
Maryport	extensive						vicus	
Burrow Walls	some							
Moresby	some							
Ravenglass	some							
Milecastles, turrets various	moderate	few			some	little		
Turf Wall	some		few		little			
Vallum	moderate		few		little	minimal		
curtain, ditches etc	some		few		minimal	minimal		

Environmental work along Hadrian's Wall

orange=major analysis, green=moderate work; yellow='something done'

DIG = excavations of all levels eg evaluations, full research etc.

	DIG	bone	seeds	bugs	pollen	soils
Ravenglass						
Moresby						
Burrow Walls						
Maryport						
Beckfoot						
Bowness						
Kirkbride						
Drumburgh						
Burgh by Sands						
Carlisle						
Stanwix						
Old Church, Brampton						
Castlesteads						
Nether Denton						
Birdoswald						
Throp						
Carvoran						
Great Chesters						
Haltwhistle Burn						
Peel Gap						
Vindolanda						
Houseteads						
Carrawburgh						
Chesters						
Corbridge						
Halton Chesters						
Rudchester						
Benwell						
Washingwells, Whickham						
Bottle Bank, Gateshead						
Newcastle						
Wallsend						
South Shields						

is a need to investigate the longevity of native settlements of the Roman period in order to throw light on what has been a longstanding gap in the settlement record extending from the third or fourth centuries AD until the appearance of nucleated villages and common field agriculture, whenever that was. This continues to be one of the most pressing unresolved problems in the archaeology of the region as a whole.

18. Installing dipwells at Vindolanda

5.3 New investigations

5.3.1 The Assessment has shown that there are large gaps in our knowledge often as a result of interventions occurring many decades or centuries before biological material, especially, was rigorously collected. New investigations need to be undertaken specifically to address the shortcomings of present knowledge. This might mean that landscape and environmental questions lead the intervention rather than the archaeology itself in some instances.

5.3.2 Biological materials that were collected and are in archives need an informed assessment. For example, the large assemblages of animal bones from South Shields and Vindolanda would benefit here and it is not even known how many collections of marine shell there are at all. Since the recovery of this material, and with the development of new techniques for study, many more questions have arisen that they could be used to address. The Carlisle Archive project undertook audit of material available from excavations within and around Carlisle, we now need to act upon that and audit the other material from the Wall.

5.3.3 Rural sites have enormous potential to address land-management issues, given the limitations of bone survival. Obviously there is a crucial chronological element in any such work too. These should reflect LPRIA and post-Roman sites as well as those contemporary with the military occupation.

5.3.4 A significant proportion of the environmental work undertaken remains unpublished; this has to be addressed.

5.4 Techniques

5.4.1 The application of LiDAR and other remote sensing techniques may pay dividends in the pasturelands of the west, or other areas where present land-use could hide archaeological evidence. However, it is essential that a suite of techniques is used rather than any one in isolation. The opportunities for - and the costs of - LiDAR therefore should be explored.

5.4.2 Application of techniques such as DNA and isotopic analyses have the potential to improve our knowledge of procurement of stock as a minimum. This will contribute to discussion of wider topics such as the impact of becoming a frontier on the landscape and how useful theoretical models of opportunity/resistance/exploitation are for landscapes.

5.5 Environmental change

5.5.1 Given future climate change forecasts, organic preservation at several sites might be placed at risk. Environmental monitoring at Vindolanda is already trying to understand the physical and chemical properties of water at the site as well as the effect that excavation itself has upon these. Such work would be of value at other sites in different present environmental envelopes, for example west of the watershed.

5.5.2 Further investigations of biological proxies in peats could provide more detailed insight into fluctuations in climate, especially at sites at the eastern end of the Wall where present evidence is minimal. Suitable deposits are not abundant but should be present even if of restricted size.

5.5.3 Existing knowledge of changes in sea level/river level and courses needs consolidation. Sea level affects the navigability of rivers, which is a major consideration for movements of troops and other commodities. This could be tied to locations, altitudes or topographic setting of bridges, for example, and help to understand the layout of some structures.

5.6 Landscape management

5.6.1 For many areas our understanding of field systems (shapes of fields, distributions, boundary types and structural materials, drove ways, relationship of fields/paddocks etc. to settlements and settlement types) is limited. Extensive remote survey, excavation and dating are required but this does not necessarily mean large projects. Several small projects could work well although overall co-ordination of methodology would be needed.

5.6.2 Map-regression studies are under-valued and under-utilised. For instance, this technique could help differentiate between second- and eighteenth-century quarries.

5.6.3 There is considerable potential for geo-archaeological studies into both river sediments and the silts that accumulated in the Vallum and Wall ditch

19. Wall in the central sector approaching Sycamore Gap

5.6.4 An essential requirement for the Roman military was an adequate and reliable supply of water. More research is needed on both supply and disposal of water. Biological materials have high potential to differentiate fresh from foul water.

5.7 Classes of material

Investigation of the various classes of material detailed below contributes to the more general questions of climate and environmental change, landscape management and procurement of resources. However, it is felt appropriate to separate out the materials since many sites will not produce them all and it is easier for specialists to think about their own materials in the first instance.

5.7.1 Animal bones

Animal bones tend to survive only in favourable ground conditions such as those where deep archaeological deposits create their own micro-habitats or where the underlying geology is alkaline. There is an area of limestone in the central area of the Wall where preservation of animal bones should be good even on relatively shallow sites, including rural settlements. This area should be targeted for excavation with particular attention to the recovery of animal remains.

5.7.2 Fish/marine

Marine and coastal resources require targeted investigation as they have often been overlooked in the past and yet provide important information about habitat exploitation and choice of resource (ethnicity could be significant here: do soldiers from inland Continental areas know what to do with a flounder?). Sites at either end of the Wall (Carlisle, Stanwix, the forts along the Cumbrian coast, South Shields, Wallsend and Newcastle) are all well placed for the exploitation of marine, inshore and estuarine resources, and many sites further inland are adjacent to rivers (eg Birdoswald). It is therefore important that explicit recovery methods are in place to test for the presence of fish bones at all sites along the Wall. It should be noted that freshwater fishes often have very small bones, and these will only be recovered by targeted large-scale bulk sediment sieving (although the mesh size can be quite coarse e.g. 1 - 2mm). Such recovery programmes would also benefit other studies e.g. the recovery or absence of very small foetal and neonatal bones of domestic livestock could indicate whether or not breeding animals were kept on site. The results would also contribute to research into aspects of military procurement.

5.7.3 Invertebrates

Invertebrates could provide further data to assist in interpreting climate, environment and living conditions. Anoxic deposits, such as those sealed by clay or waterlogged, should be extensively and intensively sampled. Due to the poor preservation conditions associated with many second- to fourth-century stone-built sites, very little invertebrate material has been recovered. For these later periods invertebrate remains are most likely to be retrieved only from isolated deposits such as deep wells and, possibly, waterlogged basal ditch deposits. These give 'spot data' and therefore preclude the spatial analyses that have been so informative for the earlier periods. They do, however, have the potential to address several important questions that cannot be addressed from the vast majority of 'ordinary' deposits, and deserve a very high priority during excavation and post-excavation. Kenward (in press) contains many recommendations for research priorities and for methods of sampling, processing and analysis.

5.7.4 Turf

Turf ramparts are common on many sites and often individual turves are clearly visible within them. These have high palaeoecological potential to determine the nature of the landscape immediately around the site.

5.7.5 Textiles

Textiles may well be considered as small finds but at least some will have been produced from locally grown fibres. Or were the fibres or textiles all imported? Pollen from suitable deposits has the potential to investigate hemp and flax cultivation and plant macrofossils the processing debris. Waterlogged native sites might be the most appropriate for targeting should any be present in the area.

5.7.6 Wood

- Wood was a vital resource but its survival is patchy. Any site with even reasonable amounts of preserved wood should be targeted for investigation.
- Technologies used in conversion of trees to structural timbers have not been well studied. Likewise the smaller wood (hurdles, wattling and so forth) should be used to investigate local climatic parameters and woodland management. This will require careful sampling and recording as it is not just a case of taking bulk samples.
- Although large timbers are regularly used for dendro chronological studies, dendro-climatological studies should be considered too.
- The question of how much wood was needed for Hadrian's Wall has not been addressed at many sites and neither is it known whether local material was adequate.
- Work on wood needs to consider whether the change from timber to stone structures could be linked to availability. Any work looking at woodlands and landscape should integrate evidence from at least wood, pollen and charcoal.
- Wood was an important fuel and ovens/hearths are abundant on many forts. Investigations of fuel debris, ie charcoal, would help investigate changing availability or sourcing of fuel.

5.7.7 Soils

- There is considerable potential for geo-archaeological studies to investigate colluviation caused by arable cultivation especially in river valleys e.g. Tyne, Solway and Eden.
- More is needed on pre-Roman and Roman ploughing - why can we only see Iron Age field systems?

5.7.8 Pollen

Pollen studies are still very much at the general vegetation change end of analysis and the emphasis should become one of addressing archaeological questions. Much more needs to be done to look at fine-scale changes especially towards the end of the Roman military presence. Such work needs a close network of sampling sites and therefore, like the application of LiDAR, requires significant resources. As a result clearly focussed questions need formulating.

A.6 Production and Procurement

Material culture from the Wall zone has been found and collected in many different circumstances and the outstanding requirement for this theme remains an assessment of the existing resource, alongside a reassessment of the published material. The quantity and potential of the material, in terms of both that originally found and the elements still available for study, is considerable and includes assemblages which are of international significance. The circumstances under which objects would arrive or be produced in the Wall zone remain only broadly understood, and then only certain types of find. Our understanding of the local economies remains modest and further work on issues that go to the very heart of our understanding of the frontier, such as cross-border trade, is essential.

6.1 Existing data

6.1.1 There is a substantial *corpus* of material relating to supply and production, including both surviving finds, and records of differing quality for those that have been lost. The assemblages from Wall sites have been analysed to varying degrees by varying techniques, resulting in some that have been published to modern standards, some that were dealt with in the past and have not been revisited and some that are trapped in the publication backlog. The necessary assessment or reassessment of this existing material must be undertaken, particularly in those cases where the assemblages have not been published. It is also desirable to re-examine the finds from early excavations that are in print to ensure that the identifications and conclusions remain robust and that their contexts were accurately interpreted.

6.1.2 It is crucial that there is dissemination of information from specialists through training and data presentation.

6.1.3 There is an absence of full, published synthetic overviews of the various find types and industrial activity current in the Wall zone. Numismatics, metalworking, faunal assemblages and samian would all benefit from such projects, which should help to clarify patterns of supply and production.

6.1.4 There is a considerable bias in the existing data towards assemblages from Roman military sites and military *vici*. Very little is known about the material culture from indigenous-style settlements.

6.1.5 Coins, pottery and tile stamps can provide securely-dated contexts, but further targeted groups remain desirable.

6.2 Local production

6.2.1 At least some of the materials required to supply the army were manufactured in the immediate hinterland of the forts. It is known that the kilns at Brampton supplied both Vindolanda and Carlisle, although in general the location of kilns in the Wall zone and the distribution patterns of their goods are little known. The precise location of the important production site at Corbridge has yet to be identified. There is a pressing need for the publication of pottery from the excavated kiln sites.

6.2.2 Small-scale metalworking is well attested in the frontier area, with military buckles and mounts known to have been produced, although whether these were manufactured by military or civilian artisans remains unclear. A number of buildings in forts have been identified as *fabricae*, but there is an absence of evidence for large-scale metalworking within them.

6.2.3 A considerable number of animals would have been required to supply and support the military units, in terms of offering a source of materials such as wool and leather, serving as transport and providing food. The extent to which such raw materials and food were imported into the zone or locally produced remains debated. Crucially there is very little knowledge of faunal assemblages from rural sites.

6.2.4 Military quarries are known to have been worked in the WHS, although few of the existing sites can be assigned to the Roman period with certainty. Whether any quarries were civilian concerns is unclear, as is the extent to which querns and whetstones were manufactured locally.

6.2.5 It is highly likely that there was change in the intensity and nature of local production over time, either as new species or skills were introduced to the area, or existing resources were exhausted. There is a need to develop methodologies so that theories, such as a shift from a reliance on importing to one of impinging on the local landscape, can be tested.

6.2.6 Given the capability of local craftsmen to work 'Roman' raw materials into 'Roman' objects, it is difficult to apply a strict definition of a 'Roman' artefact. This also impedes any attempt to differentiate between 'indigenous' and 'Roman' production in the frontier zone. The trade in 'souvenirs' represented by the Rudge Cup and its counterparts should perhaps be seen in this light, while the analysis of such artefacts and other exotica in general would benefit from further research.

6.3 Imports

6.3.1 A wide range of objects in everyday use in the Wall zone were transported from production sites outside the region. The ceramic goods best demonstrate the multiplicity of different sources, although wooden goods (or perhaps more accurately their contents) and exotic foodstuffs are known to have travelled from southern England or the continent. The origins of and routes by which many other commodities arrived in the Wall zone remain unclear.

6.3.2 Samian is one of the longest studied indexes of trade and exchange in the Wall zone, but there are biases in the existing data. Historically most attention has focused on stamps and decoration, at the expense of fabric, incidence by form and plain forms.

6.3.3 The study of coins from the WHS also has a long history. Despite this there is no modern catalogue of hoard finds from the region. The detailed study of material that permits a direct comparison between numismatic patterning in forts and their extramural settlements remains desirable.

6.3.4 The well-dated occurrence of a range of coarse wares in the Wall corridor indicates that changes in supply could be sudden and radical. It remains vital that all pottery is quantified and published to modern standards. There is a lack of well-dated groups from the first three quarters of the fourth century.

6.3.5 The majority of amphorae in the frontier zone appear to have contained olive oil. There is potential for lipid analysis to test this.

6.4 Mechanisms and patterns of production and supply

6.4.1 There were a range of circumstances by which supplies could arrive in the Wall zone or be produced within the region. The balance and relationship between commercial, entrepreneurial and military/official supply continues to be unclear, although study of this aspect has been considerably advanced by the details recorded on writing-tablets. However, questions concerning the scope and nature of military contracts are ongoing. Equally, items were also sent by relations, and heirlooms or domestic/status items could be carried in by individuals or acquired on route. Such unofficial transfer of materials provides a particular challenge, and can also be linked to questions of ethnicity versus trade, where the notion that finds can identify different populations is fundamental.

6.4.2 Local Traditional Ware (LTW) offers the potential to provide an insight into trade between the indigenous population and military garrisons, while petrology could be used to determine its source. Equally, torbanite and shale is known to have come from sources north of the Wall. Beyond this, the extent to which there were developed trading relations between the military and the indigenous population, both north and south of the Wall, and the nature of it remains uncertain. Without further details from rural sites it is impossible to reconstruct the local economies either before or after the conquest.

6.4.3 It has been suggested that the differences apparent in the material culture present in the Roman military sites to the East and West of the Wall point to different supply systems serving these regions. An analysis of the extent of divergence in material culture between East and West is highly desirable.

6.4.4 There is scope for an examination of differences in material culture occurring between those periods when the Wall was fully occupied and those when the army had returned to Scotland. There is also the question of the extent to which we can detect changes in garrison and track their movements from changing traditions visible in their finds assemblages. This is also relevant to the determination of ethnicity through cultural indicators, such as the presence of specialised pottery necessary for a specific form of cuisine.

6.4.5 Important work has been undertaken on variations in assemblages from different structural types. Building on this, more research is needed on the applicability of 'site signatures', to determine and test the different assemblages typical for specific types of site.

6.4.6 There is more that can be learnt about modes of exchange. The quantity of coins from the Wall zone suggests a monetary economy within the Roman period, although the extent to which this extended to the rural population and the contemporary role of barter remain unclear. This is also unlikely to have been constant over time, although 'market-place' coin distributions suggest vibrant activity in the fourth century.

6.4.7 At least some barrels and other containers appear to have been reused in the frontier zone. There is potential for the study of reuse of other materials, with additional work on the secondary usage of leather remaining desirable.

A.7 Life and Society

It is clear from inscriptions that the frontier zone had a rich, multicultural population with inhabitants drawn from a wide variety of regions and classes. Stable isotope and DNA analyses of osteological material from the Wall offer an important opportunity to see whether the extant epigraphic record is representative of those that were buried in the frontier zone.

Little is known about the extent to which the military occupation brought oppression or new economic opportunities for the indigenous population, including those both already living in the frontier zone and elsewhere in the province. Other fundamental questions include the nature of the religious landscape and the influence that the beliefs of Roman servicemen had upon it. Further work on these aspects can be expected to yield results of the utmost importance and provide a tantalising insight into the human experience of life and death in the frontier zone.

7.1 Locating the resource

7.1.1 There is only detailed excavation evidence for extramural activity at a handful of sites. However, geophysical survey has revealed that such settlements were much larger than was initially suspected. Even with the considerable increase in knowledge that these surveys have furnished, some major gaps remain. In particular the majority of cemeteries for all of the groups living within the WHS during the timescale of this framework remain unlocated. Stable isotope analysis from unburnt bone provides information about the geographical area within which people grew up, while museum holdings would provide a ready source of suitable material. DNA samples can be used to investigate biological relationships and furnish information about whether incomers or locals or both were having the children. However, this technique remains expensive. Even in those cases where the locations of the cemeteries have been detected, their chronological development remains unclear.

7.1.2 It remains uncertain how many of the new Roman structures were green-field developments and how many overlay earlier settlement. This element is of particular interest when considering the urban zones. The ritual landscape is only poorly understood throughout all the periods under consideration, but would have had an everyday significance to all those living and working in the region. How did the cults and religious sites that develop in the Wall zone relate to the special places of indigenous peoples? In southern Britain, Roman shrines and temples often developed at the sites that were significant prior to the arrival of the Romans (hilltops, springs, etc.) - is the same true with the sacred sites of the Wall area? Equally the sites of local meeting places are unknown. Landscapes of resistance and the need to understand society further north has been identified as particularly valuable to notions of the function of the Wall.

7.2 Existing data

7.2.1 The Life and Society theme benefits from an accumulated wealth of data capable of re-analysis, which

20. Reconstructed gateway at South Shields

also provides an opportunity to test new theories. However, early and late material within this corpus remains hard to isolate and date, particularly in those periods where there is a shortage of diagnostic material culture. Equally, despite some important recent work there remains a strong bias in the existing data towards military activity, and an equally strong bias away from the indigenous population.

7.2.2 It would be timely to re-examine critically a range of accepted theories, such as the attribution of fort names, to ensure that the evidence is sufficiently robust to support existing interpretations.

7.3 Defining population types

7.3.1 There has been little development of models of 'Roman and Native' within the frontier zone, while the use of such terms has been criticised as both simplistic and restrictive, so that formulating a way to move beyond this terminology remains desirable.

7.3.2 The extent to which different groups can be traced through the archaeology requires further research. Determining the presence of and accommodation dedicated to certain groups, such as slaves, challenges existing methodologies.

7.4 Interaction

7.4.1 Little is known about interaction between the army and the indigenous population. Three generations after the Sarmatians arrived at Ribchester there is still a local liaison officer, although the extent to which this was exceptional is unknown. Issues such as whether units started to recruit locally, or continued to recruit from abroad are also unresolved. It has been proposed that 'local' and 'army' can be perceived as two parallel universes that only occasionally impinged, such as through taxation. However it should be stressed that such interaction need not have been one-sided and that locals could also exploit soldiers. Alternatively, the frontier has been interpreted as part of a broader attempt to foster a provincial (or 'Roman') identity, suggesting that locals would not have continued as before. There is a need to devise tests for models such as these. Parallel to this is the requirement to determine how separate forts and military *vici* were. Questions remain about who the *vicani* were and whether they had any direct links with the indigenous population, or arrived with the army and depended on them. Given the size that some of the *vici* achieved, it has been questioned at what point a fort became an adjunct to a town and what the consequences of this were. How cosmopolitan the urban areas at Corbridge and Carlisle were remains highly pertinent. If Carlisle was a *civitas* then this could imply an element of indigenous involvement, which may have implications for our perception of interaction in the wider frontier zone.

7.4.2 It would be advantageous to reassess the material from the indigenous settlement at Milking Gap, while at the same time supplementing it with further research on similar sites. There is a need to address questions concerning the extent to which resettlement occurred as a consequence of building the frontier. When, or if, this occurred the state would have had a legal obligation to provide compensation, although this is not currently identifiable archaeologically.

7.4.3 The use of pottery from a native perspective is an area which would benefit from further research. If the west is aceramic in the pre-Roman period, to what extent did the indigenous population need to adopt Roman pottery?

21. Relief of three water nymphs from Coventina's Well Carrawburgh

7.5 Modes of activity

7.5.1 It is not known how many of the gods with Celtic names in the frontier zone demonstrate continuity with the pre-Roman period and how many were imported by the auxiliaries - Coventina, for instance, is also known in France and Spain. Local *Genii* were respected. The cult of *Veteres* is well attested by inscriptions on the frontier, but debate about whether it is Germanic or local in origin continues, as do questions relating to whom or even how many gods are referred to.

7.5.2 There are various indications that education occurred in the Wall area, but few details.

7.5.3 Excavation is required in order to determine the range of activities undertaken within military *vici* and the nature of change over time. In particular the impact of the apparent abandonment of military *vici* in the third century on life and society in the Wall zone is only incompletely understood, but of fundamental importance.

A.8 The Post-Roman Archaeology of Hadrian's Wall AD 400-1000

As with the pre-Roman Agenda, the focus of this framework on the Roman-period remains means that the post-Roman theme concentrates on the immediate aftermath of the military occupation. However, this is a historical distinction rather than an archaeological one and the date and impetus for 'the end' of Hadrian's Wall as a cohesive frontier system remains uncertain. What is certain is that important changes were underway in the fabric of military occupation in the late period, with some possibly occurring as early as the mid fourth century. It is essential that further data are collected for the study of this crucial transitional period, a need that is highlighted by the NERRF and NWRRF.

8.1 Locating the resource

8.1.1 A considerable challenge is ascertaining how best to target the post-Roman resource. While immediately post-Roman occupation is attested at Birdoswald, Carlisle, South Shields and Vindolanda, its wider distribution remains a matter for debate, though links between Roman forts and post-Roman settlement and activity are seen in other parts of northern England, for example at Catterick, Binchester and Piercebridge. Even within forts there is no clear indication of where immediately post-Roman structures or activity are most likely to be concentrated. A further intangible is the extent to which damage to or the destruction of late levels at some sites, due to processes such as ploughing, has distorted our perception.

8.1.2 There is a scattering of post-Roman material along the Wall dating to the early medieval period, although the implications of such deposits are still unclear. In particular it remains unknown whether these assemblages coincide with the appearance of incoming Germans or newly fashionable locals.

8.1.3 Of particular importance is the relationship between the late-Roman military landscape and the establishment and endowment of the earliest Anglo-Saxon religious houses. What is the relationship of the original land-holdings of these churches (as far as they can be reconstructed) with territories attached to forts? How was the control of territory exercised between the end of Roman rule and the beginning of the Anglo-Saxon hegemony?

22. Lanercost Priory

8.1.4 The extent of medieval activity along the Wall remains largely unexplored. Establishment and expansion of ecclesiastical foundations are notable in the eastern and western lowlands, for example at Hexham and Lanercost, but there is very limited evidence for activity in the central upland sector until the fourteenth century, when references to brigands are found in documentary sources.

23. Reused Roman masonry in the Hexham church crypt

8.2 Interpreting the end

8.2.1 Conceptualising 'The End' remains a primary concern. It is still uncertain whether it followed a period of gradual transformation or was the product of a single event. Determining whether an event or non-event narrative should be adopted would aid understanding of both the prelude to and the aftermath following the end of the frontier. The role of danger and conflict in the frontier zone in the immediate post-Roman period is equally obscure. Views of 'The End' are fundamentally dependent on the interpretation of the material culture in relation to the presence of the military, local militias, or squatter occupation following a military withdrawal.

8.2.2 At the most basic level, the changing character and nature of function of the frontier in the post-Roman period requires investigation. The questions of if, why and when the forts were abandoned are fundamental to this, but remain open. There is a complementary need for further research on the changing nature of buildings within forts, as well as abandonment and collapse. Work is also required on whether it was only the forts that retained a post-Roman role or if other frontier and landscape features were occupied.

8.2.3 Pollen studies indicate a general stability of cleared land (with the implication of maintained levels of agriculture) through the fourth and fifth centuries, with a decline in clearance not occurring until the sixth century. While this would be consistent with a continuation of rural settlement, there is currently no structural evidence for this. It would also be useful to compare the fortunes of the forts that were in urban environments to those that were in more isolated locations.

24. Aerial photograph of the 1990 Birdoswald excavation

8.2.4 Ascertaining the significance of late layers is not straightforward. 'Dark earth' occurs at some sites, but not others and as elsewhere is still poorly understood. It is known to have accumulated at Carlisle, but apparently independently of ruins and rubbish, and the implications of this remain unclear. 'Dark earth' is known to have formed elsewhere through both the deliberate introduction of new soil and the accumulation of refuse. The most pressing requirement is to determine which of these processes determined its presence in each case and the nature of occupation or abandonment that it represents. Geoarchaeological analyses have considerable potential here.

8.2.5 Roman material culture may have continued in use into the fifth century and beyond the historic or political break with the Roman Empire. Due to the lack of such material being superseded by distinct fifth-century artefacts, the dating of archaeological layers may be conservative, resulting in a false short chronology rather than the identification of a more prolonged period of occupation.

8.2.6 There is a need for further research on land ownership in the post-Roman centuries as well as the chronology and dynamics that led to the removal and reuse of the fabric of the frontier and its installations. In particular it would be desirable to reappraise the shielings and other agricultural buildings in order to determine their date and how they relate to the robbing.

8.3 Chronology

8.3.1 Chronology remains a major concern. On a conceptual level there is the need for a consensus governing when the post-Roman period begins, with dates of c. 350 and c. 410 having been proposed.

8.3.2 Directly dating the archaeological layers also represents a considerable challenge, as stratified sequences continue beyond the manufacture of the last Roman artefact. This is compounded by the absence of a diagnostic fifth-century material culture, though basic reassessments of existing data suggest some trends in the material culture developing in the later fourth century and seemingly continuing into the fifth century.

8.4 Supply and material culture

8.4.1 It is unclear what became of the supply network in the post-Roman period. Fundamental changes to this would have impacted directly on the relationship between the inhabitants of the Wall zone and the state, as well as the frontier and its landscape. Determining the character of such a shift in the regional economy, as well as clarifying any changing use of coins and pottery would facilitate the provision of a wider framework into which the existing excavation evidence could be integrated.

8.4.2 Patterns of trade may also have shifted. There is an apparent absence of imported B- and E-wares from Carlisle. The implications of this remain uncertain, but if there was restricted access to imported ceramics, this could well prove pertinent to our perception of Carlisle's role within the post-Roman landscape.

8.4.3 The specifics of material culture in the immediate post-Roman period require clarification. Evidence that indicates there was a shift to a more simplified suite of material culture is beginning to accrue, with specialised tools giving way to knives, and a range of tablewares being replaced by jars. There may also have been a broader use of more readily available organic materials, including antler. Any such decrease in the variety of material culture and availability of materials has important connotations for our understanding of this period.

RESEARCH STRATEGY

S.1 Introduction and Key Universal Priorities

The Research Strategy is intended to respond to the gaps in knowledge highlighted in the Agenda by devising a prioritised set of objectives and outlining the means by which they can be delivered. Such an undertaking is by necessity a point-in-time exercise and it is anticipated that provision will be made for the recommendations in this section to be revisited at 5-year intervals. If the exercise has been a success, then this portion of the framework will require substantial revision. This will also provide an opportunity to assess whether progress is consistent across all the themes or if a change in emphasis is necessitated. Following discussion amongst the archaeological community, it was decided that the current Strategy should be planning for the next 5 years, but also looking to 30 years. As such, both short-term and longer-term objectives are discussed in this section. It is also important to note that many of the interpretative questions identified in the Agenda have been challenging scholars for over a century and as such cannot be answered by a single project or analysis. Equally, as the Agenda has demonstrated, the gaps in knowledge pertaining to the archaeology of the Wall corridor are many and varied. Any attempt to resolve all of these within a 5- or even 30-year period would be unfeasible and accordingly not every aspect of the Agenda will be addressed directly here. It should also be stressed that the Strategy is intended to actively promote research rather than impede new ways of thinking and that it must be sufficiently flexible to take full advantage of new opportunities or developments, including making maximum research use of development-led projects. The priorities and projects discussed in the Strategy represent the consensus view of the Hadrian's Wall archaeological community and stakeholder groups.

25. Excavations at South Shields

The Strategy outlines projects and recommendations that present opportunities for participation or require action at a range of levels. In some cases an awareness of the issues and the adjusting of existing methodologies to cater for them is all that is necessary. Where small interventions are required, both developer-driven or purely research excavations could provide the data needed and in such cases it would seem desirable to concentrate research funding in those areas which are least likely to be supported by developer-funding. However, many of the Agenda items, such as those relating to extramural settlement and cemeteries, demand area excavation at sites which are unlikely to be subject to developer-led interventions. Such initiatives would touch on Agenda items in many if not all of the thematic groups and require considerable funding to undertake, analyse and disseminate the results of the exercise. A range of potential funding bodies exist, although eligibility varies and, of course, in all cases competition is fierce. The Wall corridor is also fortunate in having long-running research excavations established at South Shields, Vindolanda and Wallsend forts, and these will continue to make major contributions to knowledge.

26. Walking the central sector of the Wall

There are instances where fresh excavation is not an integral element of the Strategy items, as there is a backlog of material from earlier work which either still needs processing to modern standards or would repay further analysis. Non-invasive techniques such as analytical field survey, aerial photography, geophysical prospecting and field-walking have repeatedly proven their worth, while there is considerable potential for map regression studies. There is the possibility that local volunteer groups could make significant contributions in some of these areas. Dialogue with those engaged in agricultural work within the WHS should also be encouraged, as farmers often know where sites on their land are, even if they cannot date them. Collaboration and communication are crucial elements here. There are also many areas where an individual researcher could make an important contribution. In many cases the particular skills and interests of the individual will be a major factor in developing their research, although the establishment of bursaries at universities to support postgraduate study of specific topics identified in the Agenda would promote the undertaking of key studies.

Although only a minority of the possible permutations of the Agenda items into the basis for masters or doctoral theses are specifically developed here, this does not mean the other topics are unimportant, or that university-based research is the only route by which individual research can make a contribution. While a range of specialisms are represented in the frontier archaeological community, techniques such as lipid and stable-isotope analyses invite collaborative research and there is an obvious advantage to making those active in these fields aware of the potential of the Wall assemblages. A wider appreciation of many specialist aspects, particularly some classes of finds, is hampered by the absence of synthetic treatments of the existing data which therefore needs to be addressed.

As such, contributions towards the delivery of the Strategy can be made at all levels, with objectives that are well suited to universities, NGOs, museums, development and control and curatorial archaeologists, contractors, community groups and independent or postgraduate researchers.

The Strategy Items

For ease of reference the eight themes utilised in the Assessment and Agenda are retained here, although many of the projects proposed for one theme would have obvious benefits for advancing knowledge of others. Where such cross-cutting occurs appropriate reference will be made. However, there are nine priorities which have been highlighted by either all or a majority of the eight themes and given their wide-ranging relevance these are outlined below.

Key Universal Priorities

I. Audit of existing material.

It has become clear that it is not always easy to establish how much work has been conducted in the WHS, whether the data and/or material generated survives, where it is held and what condition it is in.

It has been observed that one of the great strengths of the Wall corridor is the scale of the archaeological resource and a full survey of the existing material would showcase the diverse and multidisciplinary research potential the Wall offers.

In order for such a project to be definitive and achievable, it is a prerequisite to know the nature of the information available. A major archive survey was commissioned by the RCHM in the late 1980s and this has been updated to 2006 for the current project (see Appendix 1). This and the more recent Carlisle Archive Project, offer a useful starting point for a more detailed and comprehensive survey . This would encompass the entire WHS area and include both interventions yet to be reported upon as well as material susceptible to forms of analysis unavailable or undeveloped when the original work was done. Much of the data would be relevant to the proposed GIS (III) and this should provide the impetus for a full treatment.

Complementary to this is a need to quantify the extent of past intervention and ascertain what percentage of Hadrian's Wall has been seen or excavated. The final figure would be expected to dispel any notion that the frontier has been over-excavated.

It would also be advantageous to establish the extent to which unpublished earthwork survey, geophysical analysis and LiDAR (see 3.1) have been conducted within the WHS, so that finite funding resources are not expended on unnecessary duplication of effort.

Once completed, such an assessment would need to be kept up to date and it has been noted that a GIS would do much of the work of a single archive. The Shoreline Management Plan for the North West has successfully assembled the metadata for the coastline, showing what is available and where it is located, in a single place and a similar arrangement for Hadrian's Wall would be highly advantageous.

27. Turret 44b and Walltown Crags

Audit of potential.

This should investigate the extent to which professionals such as education officers and community archaeologists have time to train community groups and run activities such as field walking and map regression studies.

II. Risk assessment for Hadrian's Wall.

A detailed risk assessment, providing a full survey of visitor threats and damage to the frontier from human activity as well as that occurring as a result of natural processes, is an essential management tool that will also help to prioritise sites for interventions. It is well known that the cemetery at Beckfoot is being eroded, and geophysical survey at Chesters has indicated that archaeological features there are being damaged by erosion to the east of the fort. English Heritage is currently examining stabilisation at

28. The robbed out remains of the Wall and Milecastle 29

Birdoswald. A desktop assessment of Ravenglass concluded that erosion is not as acute as was feared in the late 1990s, with denudation being episodic rather than constant, and where a highly significant amount of information relating to the fort was salvaged by 'rescue' excavation in the 1970's. Elsewhere visitors have worn gate thresholds smooth, inhibiting their study. Comparable damage is likely elsewhere and must be identified and assessed. Unconsolidated and unexcavated stretches of the Wall are particularly vulnerable and it is essential that tourism is carefully managed to ensure the long-term sustainability and integrity of the archaeological resource.

In those cases where sites are actively threatened, appropriate mitigation should be undertaken either to prevent damage or ensure that as much as possible is learnt about the archaeological features before they are lost or irreparably damaged. Where possible such rescue excavations should attempt to target items in the Agenda, with the erosion of the Beckfoot cemetery providing an opportunity to follow up work already conducted and gather important data pertaining to both burial practices and ethnicity (see 7.2 and 7.4).

III. Development of a layered Hadrian's Wall Geographic Information System (GIS).

A comprehensive GIS is an essential research and management tool. Its development would require a number of practical issues to be overcome, including difficulties associated with hosting, accessibility, maintenance, licensing for some datasets (e.g. OS, BGS), and funding (both capital and revenue). The latter consideration makes a partnership inevitable and the possibility of collaboration between Hadrian's Wall Heritage Ltd. and English Heritage should be explored.

It has been emphasised that a machine plan is not sufficient and that a proper contour record is needed. The GIS needs to be able to work as a 3D model capable of testing intervisibility and predicting the location of new sites through view-shed analysis. It is essential that the results of the NMP and rectified APs feed into it. Equally, there are repeated references to databases in this Strategy and these should all be linked into the GIS. Wherever possible these data must be 3D with a methodological focus on getting the right information, rather than the cheapest. Much of the work advocated in 'I' would need to be undertaken as preparatory work for the GIS.

If the GIS is to give full coverage to aspects such as the Stanegate, its scope must not be constrained by the boundaries of the WHS. The community needs to define the area of study as well as the purpose and end-users of the resource. This detailed discussion could be undertaken by the proposed Hadrian's Wall Forum (see VIII). The undertaking of a feasibility study would be an obvious first step for such a project.

IV. Chronology.

The inadequate chronological information available for almost all of the features within the frontier zone remains a fundamental limitation. This affects all of the themes, though in varying ways. Very few of the features which appear to be Iron Age or Roman Iron Age on morphological grounds have been independently dated, while little is known of the chronology of many landscape features or changes. Without this knowledge it is impossible to place sites within their landscape context or assess socio-economic changes over time. More work is needed on dating late-Roman and post-Roman deposits, while many questions remain about those areas where a basic chronological framework does exist, particularly the Stanegate sites and the Wall. One essential requirement that could have a major impact is to incorporate the need to undertake multiple scientific dates - provided suitable material is present - into project specifications when archaeological interventions may include pre- or post-Roman features. Many of the strategies proposed in this section would also provide valuable chronological data, with 1.6, 1.7, 1.8, 2.3, 2.4, 2.5, 2.6, 3.1.3, 3.2, 3.3, 3.5, 3.7, 4.2, 5.1, 5.2, 6.9, 6.11, 7.2, 7.3, 7.4, 7.7, 8.1.1, 8.3 particularly likely to enhance our chronological control (see also IX).

V. Communicating knowledge, raising awareness and improving public understanding.

The quantity and nature of unpublished material from the Wall zone varies from theme to theme, while the current status of the material is not uniform, creating a range of challenges.

Substantial progress has been made towards finalising the writing-up of those earlier excavations where a sufficiently comprehensive archive exists to make publication viable. Many of these are now ready for publication. However, full reports are still awaited from some more recent and completed programmes of excavation. The dissemination of results from excavations conducted to modern standards has the potential to advance knowledge of the greatest range of topics. It is crucial that resources are made available to write-up such material and where appropriate funding for research assistants or the equivalent should be sought.

Unpublished reports, often on small-scale interventions and termed 'grey literature' are a serious concern. These reports lie in three separate HERs and are known to include important material yet to be fully analysed and interpreted, including data from geophysical surveys. Major excavations and key stratified finds sequences need to be more widely accessible if the information contained within them is to be used to its full potential. OASIS provides an online index for grey literature in England and Scotland, while some project archives are available through the Archaeology Data Service. There is an annual round-up of grey literature in the West, and a similar arrangement in the East is desirable. An easy and reliable means of establishing where work has been undertaken is a fundamental requirement and a web resource specifically catering for Hadrian's Wall should be developed to keep people informed as to where interventions are underway in the frontier zone. A university would be well placed to host this.

Publications such as the annual *Archaeology County Durham* and *Archaeology in Northumberland* magazines have proved to be a popular way to circulate details of PPG16 and research excavations in the county and the feasibility of an equivalent publication spanning the frontier zone should be explored. In addition, an annual Hadrian's Wall Archaeology Day, organised on similar lines to those held by county council archaeology services throughout

29. Unexcavated Wall west of Great Chesters

England, could be held where the results of recent work in the frontier zone could be communicated to a broad audience, raising the profile of Hadrian's Wall as an area at the forefront of archaeological research.

There are sometimes difficulties associated with securing publishers for earlier excavations written up in recent years. Electronic publication is becoming increasingly popular and there are circumstances where this is the most appropriate form of dissemination, although in such instances there should be an obligation to publicise its existence, ensure that accessibility is as easy and inclusive as possible and make provision for its long-term sustainability/survival. The internet also offers considerable potential to disseminate data in all its forms. A variety of projects are using it as a means by which researchers can access raw data and the proposed Hadrian's Wall GIS could make a wealth of datasets available in this way.

VI. Access to Knowledge.

The promotion of general access to knowledge about Hadrian's Wall amongst all of those individuals and groups with an interest in both the World Heritage Site as designated and the physical monument itself with its related structures and features is a key priority.

The aim should be to produce information at a level where it is accessible by both academic and non academic 'researchers' such that it might:

- stimulate the development of a range of research projects contributing towards the delivery of the overall aims of both the HWR Strategy and Framework.

- turn passive consumers of 'expert' information into producers of their own valid knowledge and ideas about all aspects of the Wall's archaeology.

The co-ordination of this aspect of the HWRF could be a central task of the Hadrian's Wall Forum (VIII), which, itself, could serve as an excellent vehicle to bring together both amateur and professional Wall devotees in a mutual two-way dialogue that would be beneficial to both groups.

VII. Specialist succession planning.

There is a need both to identify specialisms that we want to develop and to be proactive in succession planning so that study continues at a level which is the same or higher than that currently. The NERRF (p 229) draws attention to the crucial need for training of small finds and pottery specialists, as well as the suitability of undergraduate and postgraduate theses to provide an introduction to these disciplines. Mentoring by more experienced individuals should form part of this, and would be in line with the knowledge transfer advocated by the government. English Heritage has funds to add value to existing projects, presenting an opportunity to pay specialists to provide training to those carrying out community excavations.

A certain skills base is needed to prepare for study at doctorate level, and representations could be made to the AHRC for this to be included in the 1 + 3 system. Retaining newly acquired skills in archaeology will to a great extent be dependent upon improvements in career structures in the profession more generally.

VIII. Hadrian's Wall Research Forum.

A body should be set up to provide an outlet for the dissemination of research undertaken, and for research opportunities and issues to be discussed amongst those concerned or interested in Hadrian's Wall. The creation of a forum would provide a mouthpiece for the community and permit others to communicate directly with it. Such a body would also be crucial for advocating the archaeological potential of the WHS to outside bodies, facilitating collaboration and taking forward the projects prioritised in the research strategy. Its very existence would assist funding applications as the relevant bodies would be able to see that there is a structure in place.

The members of this forum must be representative of the various paid and non-paid archaeologists, academic researchers, local societies and wider community interests. As a first step the precise structure and scope, including its relationship to existing bodies such as the Hadrian's Wall World Heritage Site Management Committee, would have to be discussed in detail and agreed by the community. One possibility would be to retain the general setup adopted for the Research Framework with a small steering group and periodic full public meetings, which appears to have been effective and well-received.

IX. Flagship strategic projects.

A series of major projects are required to tackle a multiplicity of Agenda items from across the thematic groups, demonstrate the research potential of Hadrian's Wall and engage the public. As well as delivering a substantial increase in knowledge and raising the profile of the Wall amongst professionals, these initiatives would seek to incorporate opportunities for community involvement and deliver on-site interpretation for visitors, and to re-invigorate the image of the Wall as an active and vibrant research resource. Projects on this scale are essential if fundamental uncertainties concerning important aspects of the frontier are to be objectively addressed. The projects in question are developed in detail within the thematic sections with which they are primarily associated. They are:

1.7/1.8 Rural settlement (Pre-Roman/Roman/Post-Roman multidisciplinary study)
3.2 Transect across the frontier.
4.2 Fort and extramural settlement.
6.3 Food and diet.
7.4 Investigation of cemeteries.

S.2 The Pre-Roman Archaeology of the Tyne-Solway Isthmus

Scope: Study of this aspect must extend beyond the boundaries of the WHS, not least because one of the key priorities identified here and in the NWRRF and NERRF is the transition between the Iron Age and Roman periods. If this is to be studied, then controls from without the immediate area will be required in order to test the extent of local and regional variety.

2.1 Survey and remote sensing.

Modern topographical and geophysical surveys of the principal known sites are necessary first steps in recording and quantifying the existing resource. It would also allow future excavations to be targeted, maximising the impact of any further funding that becomes available. Warden Hill was identified as a potentially extremely important site, fully deserving of survey and geophysics as a minimum.

2.1.1 Aerial survey.

Provision for regular aerial survey is advocated in the NWRRF. Given this technique's proven suitability for detecting sites of all periods in the region, together with the annual fluctuations in crop-mark visibility, resources should be made available for such reconnaissance whenever the conditions are appropriate. While follow-up work is, of course, required if these features are to be firmly dated, aerial survey can cover huge swathes of the landscape comparatively quickly and yield results which it would be extremely laborious to achieve any other way. More cost-effective forms of aerial surveillance are being pioneered, including attaching cameras to remote-control aircraft, and this could be explored as a cheaper means of monitoring known sites. The potential of LiDAR for revealing sites masked by later ground disturbance has recently been demonstrated in dramatic fashion by the discovery of a hitherto unknown marching-camp beside the fort at Carrawburgh.

2.1.2 Calibration of surveys.

Different types of survey should be calibrated so that the results can be interrogated and do not end up as simply dots on a map. What is required is for data to be available as layers in a GIS capable of interrogation. The GIS advocated in III would present the ideal medium for this. Are gaps indicative of the absence of settlement in the prehistoric period or attributable to changing agricultural practices or geology? The results of this exercise would assist in informing desk-based assessments.

2.2 The survival of pre-Roman horizons under later features.

Well-preserved prehistoric features have been found underlying a number of Roman sites in the frontier zone, including the Vallum at Denton (Bidwell and Watson 1996). While the Vallum mounds had been ploughed almost flat, the prehistoric soil survived intact underneath. In this context the Roman remains provide a useful and closely datable horizon. When developing research strategies or contractor briefs, it is essential to make provision for the potential size of the pre-Roman resource and maximise the research potential of PPG16.

30. Warden Hill overlooking the North and South Tyne

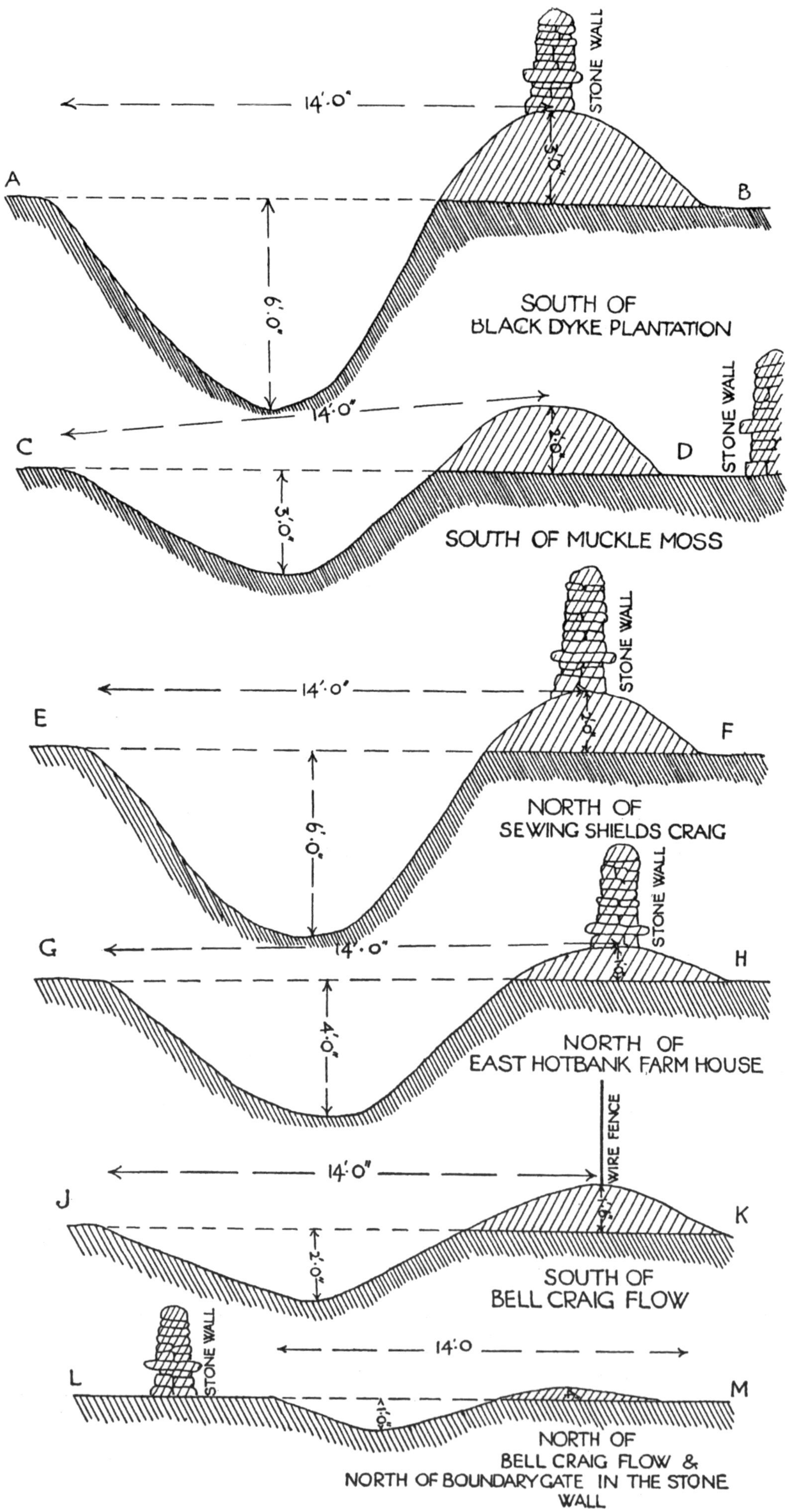

31. Sections through the Black Dyke

Although the South Shields roundhouse had been abandoned for centuries before the construction of the Roman fort, the field systems beneath Wallsend fort and the remains at Denton highlight the potential of features sealed below the earliest Roman levels to investigate the Iron Age / Roman transition at close quarters.

A proper appreciation of the pre-Roman deposits is not always achievable in keyhole trenches, and full area excavation of these features is to be encouraged.

2.3 Synthesis of the existing material.
A more detailed synthesis of the existing material (published and unpublished) than was possible for the Framework Assessment is required.

2.4 Promotion.
While the potential of the pre-Roman resource is considerable, it is often overshadowed by the Roman-period remains. The existence of outstanding, multi-period remains within the Wall corridor should be actively promoted to potentially interested parties that can access research funding, such as universities. There is considerable scope for partnerships involving these institutions, and capitalising on the range of talents in the different departments within them. Initiatives of this kind may appeal to the AHRC. In general, there is a need and desire for greater communication between prehistorians and Romanists, in particular when it comes to modelling tribal structures.

2.5 Chronology.
The inability to date accurately the vast majority of sites which on morphological grounds appear to be Iron Age in date is a fundamental limitation. Robust dating evidence is a prerequisite to distinguish between Iron Age and Roman potentially post-Roman rural settlement (see also IV, 1.6 and 1.7).

2.6 Area excavation of a late-pre-Roman settlement.
Given the scale of chronological concerns for this theme a suitable site would need to be selected on morphological grounds. There would be a clear advantage to targeting a site where the abandonment deposits are least likely to be disturbed. Once a site is chosen, accurate dating is a priority and modern scientific techniques must be used to full advantage. C14 can be used to great effect, but a large number of samples are needed - ideally 20 to 30. Alternatively, if a waterlogged site were identified, this may provide dendrochronological dates, as well as environmental indices. As developer-driven archaeology is most heavily concentrated at the eastern end of the Wall, a research excavation should consider the western sector. The repeated indications of an east - west divergence across the Tyne - Solway corridor makes it important that all of the data are not concentrated in one region. Work in the west may permit regeneration or development money to be tapped and would provide important information into the immediate context of a branch of the frontier that is all too often neglected. Obviously, it is vital to have data-sets of comparable size and type from a number of sites along the entire frontier frontier.

Research of this nature would be instrumental in developing models that can then be tested by developer-driven/rescue archaeology in the region. This would permit curators/HE officers to be specific about what is needed from a site when devising developer briefs.

2.7 Revisit Jobey sites and assemblages.
The existing information relating to the structural evidence from the prehistoric and Romano-British sites excavated by George Jobey should be reliable, so a cheaper alternative to area excavation would be to develop a project to gather material for modern dating/scientific analysis from sites previously excavated by Jobey but where suitable samples are likely to survive.. This presents considerable potential as an affordable opportunity to gather chronological data from a range of widely distributed sites. The results would be invaluable when attempting to understand the impact of the arrival of Rome on the indigenous population in what became the border zone. Jobey's work had a North East bias and so would need to be balanced against additional work in the West, ideally including sites north of the Wall.

There is a real value to looking at Iron Age sites *en masse* as large numbers of radiocarbon dates from a wide range of sites may well start to give an important indication of socio-economic trends. Any assessment of this would require data from sites beyond the immediate frontier zone, to act as a control against any changes that were occurring independently of the development of a border.

2.8 Unravelling of landscape stratigraphies.
Well-preserved multi-period palimpsest landscapes exist within the WHS, although few of the features have been directly dated and the attribution of some field systems, for instance, to discrete periods is not secure. There is a need to move from excavating sites to excavating landscapes and dating evidence for the Black Dyke would be particularly valuable. Future work into landscape stratigraphies should build on the results of the NMP survey, while the implementation of a number of the initiatives identified in the Strategy have the potential to facilitate studies of this aspect. See 4.2 in particular.

S.3 The pre-Hadrianic Frontier on the Tyne-Solway Isthmus and the Stanegate

Scope: only certain stretches of the Stanegate fall within the WHS boundaries and accordingly if the Strategy for this theme is to be all-encompassing, it must take a wider perspective.

3.1 Locating the Stanegate.
Establishing further details about the course of the road (including service roads) and the position of the associated installations is essential. This should draw on all appropriate techniques, including LiDAR, aerial photography, field-walking and predominantly small-scale trial trenching. North - south links should also be included, to ensure that our focus on the east - west alignment is proportionate to the wider system. Further details ought to assist in testing recent theories about the position of the road in the construction order. Three camps, at Fell End, Markham Cottage 1 and Seatsides 1 lie on the course of the Stanegate and geophysical survey and excavation are required to clarify their interrelationship with the road (see also 4.5). The suite of different techniques proposed means that there is plenty of scope for the inclusion of community groups and volunteers alongside professionals. The provision for annual aerial survey advocated in 1.1.1 would complement a survey of this kind. See also 3.3.

3.2 Geophysical survey.
As a minimum requirement all major Stanegate sites, including the fortlets, and their immediate surroundings should be subjected to geophysical analysis. The resulting plans have already proven to be indispensable research and management tools for those installations so surveyed. Corbridge and Nether Denton would be expected to produce particularly important results. Burgh III and Burgh I are also a desirable targets, as it should help to resolve the debate about whether the former feature is a fort or camp and also clarify the possible traces of a *principia* claimed to have been seen from the air.

3.3 A multi-disciplinary survey of the Stanegate in its landscape setting.
An investigation of how the Stanegate and its installations relate to both the pre-existing indigenous landscape and the physical topography is needed. The work of the NMP provides a starting point. Although only certain stretches of the Stanegate fall within the NMP survey area, including those on 1:10,000 map sheets NY66NE, NY76NE and NY86NE, the results will provide some indication of the potential information yield from landscape survey. Even in these areas the problem of dating features remains acute, as their significance can only be gauged if their chronological relationship with the Stanegate is understood. Field-walking may give a provisional indication in some instances. Analysing the interaction of the Stanegate with the landscape will be facilitated by the development of a GIS (See III).

3.4 Modern excavation of a smaller structure.
The fortlets and towers on or associated with the

32. Aerial photograph of Corbridge

33. Carlisle fort Period 6C

Stanegate form a crucial component of the proposed Trajanic frontier. However, the existing dating evidence is insufficient to assign the fortlets to the Hadrianic of Trajanic periods with any certainty. While a clearer indication of date would be difficult to achieve without a highly fortuitous discovery, such as an inscription, a programme of modern area excavation is overdue. The fortlets at Throp, Haltwhistle Burn and Castle Hill, Boothby all display considerable potential, while the geophysical survey advocated in 3.2 would serve to refine the options. The extant plan of Haltwhistle Burn reveals an unusual internal layout and excavation photographs indicate that a considerable proportion of the internal deposits were left *in situ*. Advances in excavation and sampling technique, and knowledge of Roman structures over the century since they were excavated provides a much greater chance of establishing the purpose of these internal buildings. This should assist in determining the function of the installation. Boothby has suffered from landslips in the past, and while it is not currently believed to be at risk, any opportunities that do arise should be used to maximum research advantage.

3.5 Survey, publication and excavation at Corbridge and/or Brampton.

Further knowledge of many aspects of the late-Roman urban centres at Corbridge and Carlisle is required. There is a need to set these urban areas within their contemporary hinterland. Both sites offer potential here, with the opportunity of developer-funded work at Carlisle to complement research at Corbridge. The Carlisle - Brampton (fort and industrial site) - Hawkhirst nexus presents an important opportunity for further fieldwork. The towns must have stimulated the development of settlement and infrastructure in their hinterland and the search for this, as well as excavation at a site such as Hawkhirst to test the potential of such settlements is highly desirable and will provide a much-needed context for the urban centres (see also 9.2). As Corbridge lies to the south of the area investigated by the National Mapping Programme, any attempt to place it within its landscape context will require additional survey. As in 3.3 this will not in itself deliver the requisite precision in chronological information.

As noted in 3.2, there is considerable potential for geophysical survey at Corbridge especially with regard to the full extent of the site and the relationship between it and the nearby fort at Red House. However many questions, including why the towns prosper after the extramural settlements decline in the fourth century, their economic basis and social make up all require further area excavation. Burials are known to the west of Corbridge and suspected to the east, providing an opportunity to examine the ethnic origins of the inhabitants (see also 8.2).

There is considerable scope for a study which sets Carlisle and Corbridge within the wider context of Romano-British urbanism. As well as providing a national perspective, considering comparanda from outside the border zone would serve as a control for the effects of development within the frontier zone on urbanism. Such a topic would be well suited to exploration in a postgraduate thesis.

3.6 The Western Stanegate: a project to re-evaluate the conclusions drawn by the late G.D.B. Jones.

34. Aerial photograph of Throp fortlet

It is believed that all of the surviving material from Prof. Jones' work on the Western Stanegate has now been published and so it is essential to undertake a project that will acquire more detailed evidence relating to the structures he identified. Elements of Jones' findings are increasingly permeating the public consciousness but cannot currently be subjected to independent scrutiny (see also 4.1.4). The opportunity must be taken to discuss his excavations with those who were involved, but ultimately further work will be required. The interim reports published by Jones, in conjunction with the NMP data, provide sufficient information for the key elements to be targeted, and excavation to test and augment existing evidence, as well as to secure material suitable for absolute dating, should produce significant results. Even if the remains prove to be non-Roman, they would still furnish important details about this area of the frontier in the period to which they belong.

3.7 The relationship of the Stanegate to the Wall.

The work of Woolliscroft (1989) and Poulter (2005; forthcoming) underlines the importance of the Stanegate to the course and construction of the Hadrianic frontier. Although it is difficult to identify formal recommendations that will shed further light on this, it is important that researchers continue to devise new ways of interrogating and testing the relationship, both initially and over time, between the Stanegate and the Wall. The proposed GIS (III) would provide a key tool for this.

S.4 The Wall

Scope: While the Wall-ditch and Vallum could be seen as demarcating the immediate border system, it would not be appropriate to restrict investigation purely to the area defined by these, not least because there may be further obstacles north of the ditch upcast.

4.1 Understanding the Wall

4.1.1 Establishing the course and survival of the Wall and its installations in Tyneside and the West.

There are a range of techniques that should be utilised to attempt to plot the precise course of the Wall and the location of its attendant installations in the West, with considerable potential for geophysical survey and LiDAR. Attempts to use geophysics to detect a number of the Wall installations in the West in 1981 achieved some success, although severe robbing in places meant that the results were mixed (Gater 1981). Modern survey may well produce clearer results, as is demonstrated by work undertaken by Timescape Research Surveys at milecastle 73 and Burgh-by-Sands (Biggins et al 2004). Greater precision is incredibly important for development control, management and future work.

35. Excavation on the line of the Wall at Wallsend

LiDAR surveys covering portions of the WHS have already been undertaken by at least two different bodies. The Environment Agency has surveyed the eastern and western ends of the Wall. This was undertaken to a high resolution and the relevant image tiles can be purchased from the Agency. Alternatively, two 2km by 2km tiles can be made available free of charge to academic students. Low-resolution non-manipulable data from the Environment Agency and covering the Solway stretch of the Wall can be consulted on the Cumbria County Council GIS. Northumberland County Council holds the area around Corbridge. English Heritage commissioned a survey of a 5km by 1.5km stretch of the Wall, centred on Carrawburgh fort and covering squares NY84 to NY88. The resulting data is believed to be the copyright of Cambridge University. The rectified image tiles can be purchased from the NMR. Resitivity could be used to test for entanglements on the berm while ground-penetrating radar would be suitable to check for re-cuts in the ditch. Geophysical surveying at milecastle 73 revealed indications of enclosures outside the installation, proving its capability as a technique to identify similar structures elsewhere (see 4.4, but also above for the wider potential shown by this work). The results of such remote sensing should then be used to target small-scale interventions, primarily to test the preservation of the structure, but with the potential to gather important data to address research questions (see 4.1.2 and 4.1.3).

36. The Wall exposed in a farm gate near Great Chesters

37. Haverfield's section through the Turf Wall

Determining the precise course of the Wall under urban Tyneside remains dependent on excavation and there is a good chance that developer-driven projects will continue to provide important details about the frontier here. The need to determine further fixed turret and milecastle locations east of turret 7b may also be resolved by work of this nature, although the difficulty with targeting these structures means that any such discoveries are likely to be fortuitous.

4.1.2 The width of The Wall.
The necessity to establish a series of secure measurements of the width of the Wall, both above and below the offsets, was identified in the Agenda and this additional aim could be integrated into a range of projects. This basic grammar of the Wall's construction is extremely important and opportunities to obtain further data may come from routine maintenance or management along the Wall, as well as developer-driven or research excavation. All such opportunities must be seized and the part of the Wall that the measurements relate to must be explicitly stated when reported in the annual *Britannia* summaries. The development of a database containing reliable and easily accessible measurements of width from sites along the entire length of the frontier would be a valuable research tool. especially with regard to determining the sequence and date of the building of individual sections of the Wall.

4.1.3 Interpreting transitions.
Much of our understanding of the building history of the Wall is dependent on changes in the material or width of the frontier curtain. However, many of these changes remain imprecisely dated. The transition from a Turf to Stone Wall and the development of the extra-Narrow Wall are, in particular, only very broadly dated. As a first step, existing unpublished material relating to this must be written up. There are also wider interpretative questions about why these changes came about and, for instance, the mechanics of slighting the Turf Wall.

While a project such as that discussed in 4.2 would provide an opportunity to investigate these issues, particularly in the western sector, a full treatment would require additional fieldwork. Much of this would overlap with other Strategy points, including the publication of excavations on the central sector (V) and re-examination of the epigraphic evidence (4.5). This programme of research should also actively seek much-needed additional data pertaining to the maintenance of the curtain in the third and fourth centuries and its survival in the post-Roman period.

4.1.4 Testing the linear barrier on the Cumberland Coast.
Attempting to resolve the many fundamental questions that remain about this stretch of frontier would necessitate a wide-ranging and long-term project (see also 3.6). One priority objective that might be achievable with a few small trenches is to test the interpretation of the linear boundary around Cardurnock. It would be appropriate to follow up the results of the NMP survey results, which indicate that similar ditches can be traced east of the termination of the Wall, between Bowness-on-Solway and Drumburgh (Boutwood 2005, 20). There are indications that one of the Cardurnock ditches was cut by tower 2b and it might be rewarding to test the junction between the parallel ditches and the milefortlet ditches.

38. The line of the Turf and Stone Walls re-merge at Milecastle 51

4.2 Transect across the frontier.
This key project will assess objectively what the Wall can yield and should be based around two transects, around 200m in length, encompassing the entire width of the frontier and beyond. Ideally, a section would be cut in both the East, allowing the original plan to be investigated, and the West, where our knowledge of the Wall structures is most restricted. This project would be most successful if it followed up the results of the geophysical and LiDAR surveys recommended above 4.1.1), which would serve to refine the

39. Milecastle 39

40. The Wall on Mons Fabricius and Highshield Crag

available options. Tough choices would have to be made about whether to target any potential areas of collapse, entanglements, ditch re-cuts, Vallum crossings, camps, indigenous settlements, specific elements of the road network or small pollen basins, depending on accessibility and desirability. If the transects were cut near forts, then this would provide a background scatter of finds.

This exercise would permit models to be developed that could then be tested elsewhere through PPG16 work. There is also potential for quite small interventions based on the findings from these large transects.

Such a project would generate considerable public interest and opportunities for engagement leading on to active research, and the publicity opportunities presented by such work must be maximised. An exercise on this scale ought only to be undertaken with the fullest possible range of community participation, ranging from collaboration with HE bodies to the involvement of local schools, groups and volunteers. Every effort should be made to make it a highly visible project as far as the public are concerned, with a comprehensive programme of interpretation on-site while the work is in progress. There is a possibility that such an initiative could be eligible for regeneration funding and is conceivably something that the Heritage Lottery Fund would support.

4.3 Reassessment of camps.
The temporary camps represent an extremely important and largely untapped resource. Area excavation of the interior and a robust absolute-dating programme are needed to shed light on the chronologies, functions (whether temporary, occupied periodically and/or for practice) and lengths of occupation at these sites. The interiors require geophysical prospecting in order to locate ovens and pits which then need to be excavated in order to recover datable material. Work at Fell End, Markham Cottage 1 and Seatsides 1 has been advocated due to their relationship with the Stanegate (see 3.1) and this would serve to test the potential knowledge yield from work of this nature.

In some cases it is not certain whether structures have been correctly identified as camps, with those concentrated in the area around Chesters causing particular concern. The analytical approach recommended above would clarify their status. There is also the potential for the discovery of new camps.

4.4 Examining the context of the smaller structures.
Magnetometry survey at milecastle 73 revealed possible traces of external enclosures and timber buildings. There are hints of extramural activity at a number of milecastles and it is desirable to conduct similar surveys at a sample of milecastles and turrets. The survey advocated in 4.1.1 could contribute to this, while other potential targets would include milecastle 19, where an altar inscription makes reference to an accompanying temple. Middens and burials may also be present. In order to assess the role and chronology of any such features, the excavation of a smaller structure and its immediate surroundings is required.

4.5 Epigraphic evidence.
The rich epigraphic legacy of the Wall has been neglected in recent years and would benefit from a comprehensive re-evaluation focusing on the evidence for building history and subsequent maintenance. Many of the building stones still need full publication and analysis, with commensurate implications for technical requirements and cost.

4.6 The Vallum.
Previous surveys of the visible remains of the Vallum should be assessed to see whether particular lengths would benefit from more intensive analytical survey. In particular, it is essential that there is a complete record of features such as gaps in the Vallum mound, ditch crossings and marginal mounds. Some experimentation with different survey and prospection methods (eg detailed contour surveys and geophysics) would be worthwhile in areas where these features are reduced or obscured by later cultivation. The proposed transects across the Wall should include large-scale excavation of the Vallum. The area to the west of Birdoswald would be well-suited to investigation of the chronology of use of the Vallum. A pilot study into the potential of coring to provide environmental indices should be conducted. See also 4.8 and 6.7

4.7 Map regression of quarries.
Despite the attention that the Wall building programme has received, there has been little detailed study of the quarries. Map regression offers clear potential when it comes to distinguishing between Roman and nineteenth-century exploitation. If the necessary training was made available, then such a project would be well suited to an interested community group or university students.

4.8 Surveying.
Recent work by Poulter has shed light on the methodology by which the courses of the Wall and Vallum were surveyed and the topographical preferences these display. His conclusion that when a straight choice was presented a southerly aspect for the Wall was preferred to a northerly one demands further study and testing (see also 3.7).

4.9 The function(s) of the Wall.
This aspect is fundamental to our appreciation of the frontier zone, but interpretations of function remain highly controversial. The problem is essentially a theoretical one and study of it should draw on ancient history, evidence-based archaeology and comparisons with frontiers elsewhere, both ancient and modern. As well as other Roman borders, there is potential for Hadrian's Wall to be studied in the context of sixteenth- and seventeenth-century architectural and documentary evidence for life in the border land, or more modern works such as the eighteenth- and nineteenth-century North Caucasus frontiers. Frontiers are increasingly relevant to the modern world, providing an important contemporary resonance for the military experience on Hadrian's Wall.

S.5 The Forts and Extramural Settlement

The ongoing research excavations at South Shields, Vindolanda and Wallsend will continue to play a major role in generating fresh data for this theme. The need for further research on a range of aspects associated with extramural settlements has been emphasised in the NERRF and by McCarthy (2002, 107).

5.1 Geophysical survey and LiDAR.

Given the massive leap in knowledge that has occurred as a result of recently conducted geophysical surveys, it is essential that the remaining sites - including the outpost forts - receive this treatment. Wherever possible, survey should also extend to the north of the frontier curtain and also directly south of the Vallum where the earliest extramural settlements are thought to have developed.

English Heritage has conducted a LiDAR survey of Carrawburgh fort (see 4.1.1) and if geophysical survey was also undertaken here, it would provide an opportunity to compare the results of these techniques in areas where earthworks survive. Although geophysical survey of a limited area outside the south-east corner of the fort in 1988 produced results that were difficult to interpret, modern techniques should produce clearer plots. Alternatively, new LiDAR survey at Housesteads or Birdoswald could be assessed alongside pre-existing geophysical plans, or the relevant tiles for Maryport could be purchased from the Environment Agency.

41. Extramural settlement at Vindolanda

5.2 Fort and extramural settlement.

Understanding of extramural settlements has been identified as a serious gap in existing knowledge and there is both a need and appetite for a major project or projects to address some of the key questions relating to these developments. These include the speed with which they developed, whether they possessed defences, and when they ceased to be occupied. Given their symbiotic relationship with the associated fort, there would be a considerable advantage to basing a project around either the examination of both elements, or targeting an extramural settlement attached to a fort that has already been subject to excavation modern standards. Important work has been recently undertaken on the extramural settlement at Vindolanda and excavation will soon commence at Newcastle. Other desirable targets include Birdoswald, Housesteads, Chesters and Maryport. Consideration should be given to the possibility that the wider context had an important impact, with potential for differences associated with whether sites were landlocked or by the sea, or even a quantifiable east - west divergence.

Comparative studies of the assemblages from forts and their extramural settlements have considerable potential to further our understanding of the nature of the relationship between these sites. Suitable material for comparisons between some find types already exists, with indications from quantified analysis of the samian suggesting marked differences in consumption. There is also potential for significant results from the numismatics from Vindolanda and Housesteads. In contrast archaeobotanical evidence has yet to be sought from extramural settlements.

A large proportion of the questions that were identified in the Agenda can only be addressed through area excavation. In particular it is crucial to follow up, give meaning to and test the interpretation of the geophysical surveys. Where structures have been detected to the north of the Wall, these should be examined and dated. Other areas to be explored include the question of zoning by status or activity, how such zoning and relationships with the fort may change through time, and the nature of temples. Equally, robust dating for the key phases of the extramural settlement, including foundation and abandonment, has been identified as a priority, as has the need to set such data within its regional, national and international context. Large-scale excavation within an extramural settlement would provide an opportunity to gather data pertinent to a range of Strategy items. A number of extramural settlements offer considerable potential for environmental sampling, for instance, while if the supposed ethnicity of the garrison is known, it would be appropriate to search for distinctive ethnic markers from that region (see also 8.2 & 8.3).

Extramural rubbish dumps remain highly desirable targets if they can be located. Any such project must, of course, allow for the possible presence of important though slight traces of post-Roman occupation (see 9).

If sufficient resources were available, then the investigation of the fort extramural settlement advocated here could run in conjunction with an investigation of the associated cemeteries. There is wide support for the investigation of burial grounds and indeed work to locate them and, just as with the extramural settlements, the most useful data would be gained from studying the cemeteries of a site which has been investigated to modern standards. See 8.2 for discussion of such a project.

5.3 Outpost forts and hinterland fort.

Although lying beyond the boundary of the WHS, the role of these installations is critical to our perception of the function of Hadrian's Wall and there are a number of outstanding questions which can only be answered by the application of modern techniques. Remote sensing is a necessary first step (see 5.1) and should confirm whether there was extramural settlement at these sites. As the forts lie outside the area examined by the NMP, any attempt to

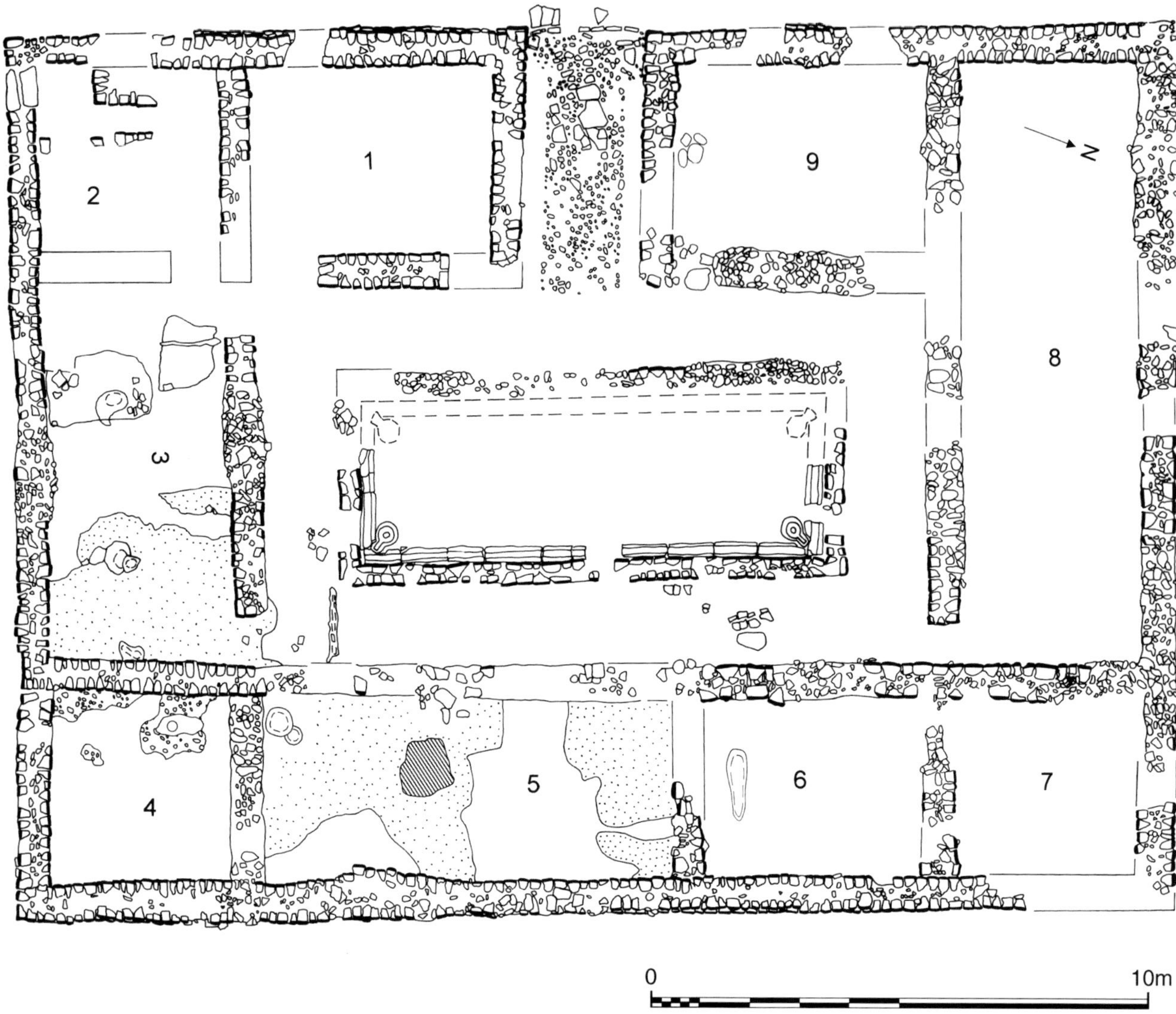

42. Excavation plan of the hospital at Wallsend

gauge their significance within the landscape and relationship to areas of indigenous-style settlement would require additional survey. Such a project, utilising the same methodology as the NMP, is highly desirable, particularly for the outpost forts. There is need for a reassessment of the numismatic and ceramic material from these sites. The final date of abandonment of the outpost forts remains unclear, although any attempt to clarify this would necessitate further excavation. There is a potential overlap with the post-Roman theme here, and Risingham has been identified as a site with considerable potential.

5.4 Internal structures and chronology.

Both general and detailed questions remain about the identification and use of internal buildings. There are queries about how securely buildings can be identified as hospitals, workshops and stores, while little work has been undertaken on the purpose of rampart-back buildings. It is time for a thorough re-evaluation of the evidence. This project must make full use of the available finds evidence to test existing theories. There is also scope to achieve a wider understanding of the use of space within these buildings. Careful analysis of the finds evidence should begin to give important insights into the nature of day-to-day activity within a *principia*. Other questions that could be addressed in this way include 'What was being made in workshops?' and 'What happened in hospitals - only medicine?' Questions of purpose are not restricted to buildings. Drainage remains poorly understood and while a pressurised water supply was sometimes provided, it is unclear for what purposes this was provided. Analysis of a range of internal structures would be well suited to a postgraduate thesis that compared the interpretation of such structures with those from elsewhere in the empire.

Unpublished material relevant to this exists, including Gillam's excavations at Halton Chesters though this is due to be published in 2009.

More details of the development of the fort internal buildings would require further excavation. Infantry barrack blocks should be considered a priority.

5.5 Perceptions of the appearance of buildings.

The frontier zone provides a wealth of well-preserved building types that represent an important resource when it comes to testing or devising virtual reconstructions of a range of military or civilian buildings in a provincial context. As well as examining how perceptions of these structures have changed over time, fragments of superstructure found during excavation or immured in later buildings can provide

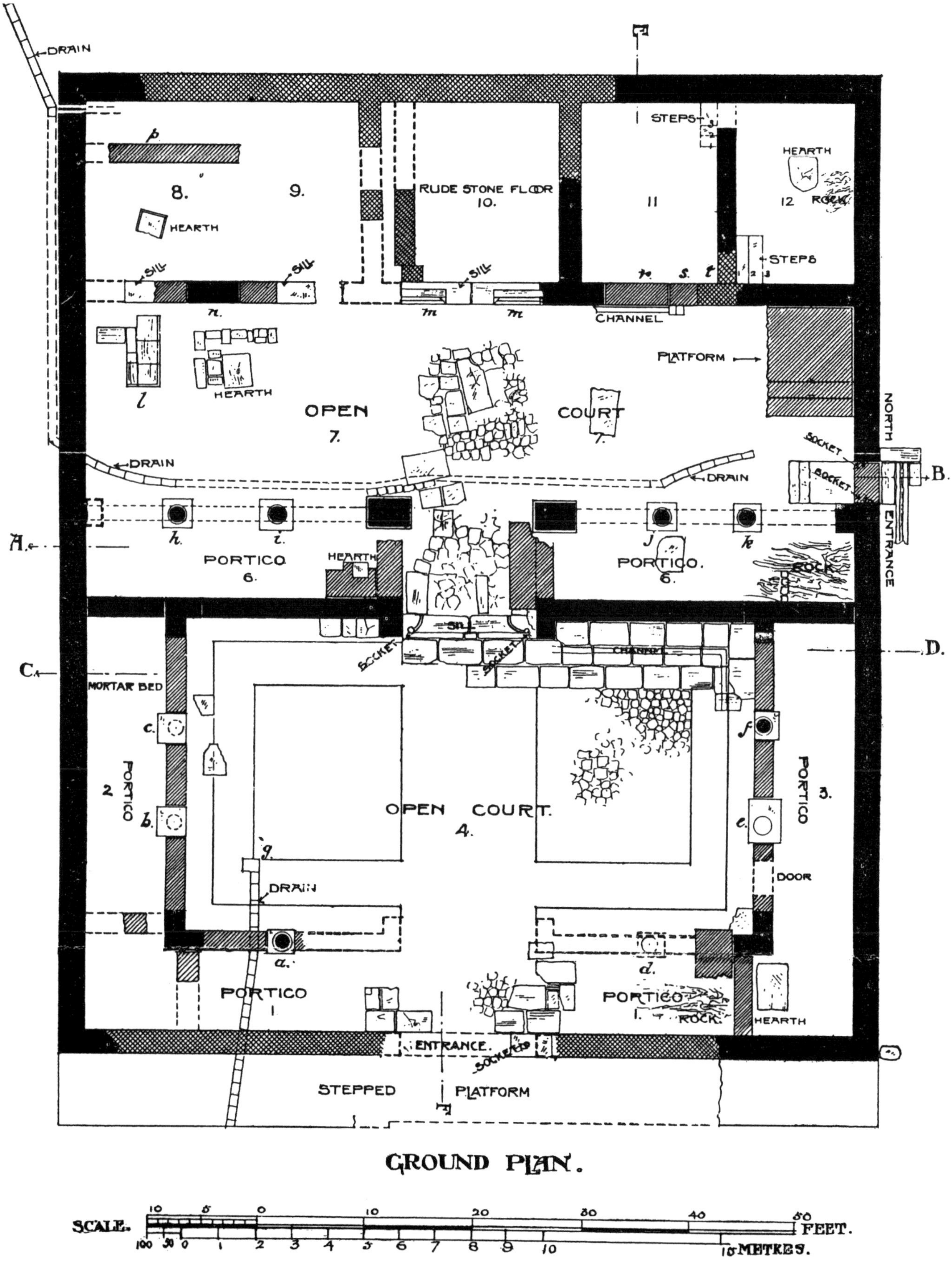

43. Excavation plan of the Housesteads principia

44. Aerial photograph of Bewcastle

important insights, as recent studies of Corbridge and the Hexham Abbey crypt have demonstrated.

5.6 Garrisons.

There is scope for a review at postgraduate level of the evidence for the presence of certain units in certain forts at certain times and also to integrate this with the structural and finds evidence. An examination of whether internal buildings, and in particular barracks vary in accordance with garrison changes, especially when this should necessitate a change in the number of soldiers, would provide interesting information on the extent to which the internal plan, and perhaps also extramural settlement, was influenced by external factors. Units from certain geographical regions may leave signatures in the form of ethnic markers such as Frisian ware or distinctive dietary habits. Further work on this aspect, and whether these markers remain constant over time, is desirable.

5.7 Attribution and meaning of fort names.

A project could examine the security with which place names have been attributed to various sites and the significance of them (why not 'Fort Augustus' or similar?).

5.8 Fort *territoria*.

A pilot study investigating the potential of map regression to provide indications of fort *territoria* should be undertaken. Presumably these were substantial, with cavalry units needing grazing for 500 horses.

S.6 Landscape and Environment

Scope: The focus has to be on the WHS but this is a very restricted area; the study zone for each topic will vary (and in many cases it will be substantially larger). This is especially true in Landscape and the Environment. In each set of proposals the authors need to be clear about the extent of their area of interest. Modification or revision of the WHS boundaries is a complex business so this is unlikely to be pursued.

The strategy should encompass both short-term and long-term timetables. Short-term aims can demonstrate the usefulness of the framework and raise its profile (especially through appropriate publication i.e. monographs or international journals). Many of the questions that were raised in the Agenda demand new excavations to answer them and these should provide new opportunities. Some are questions that are clearly achievable; others are important but their achievability is doubtful, e.g. tribal geographies through time, or any shift in the location of tribal centres.

45. Fozy Moss

6.1 Chronology.

Crucial and fundamental, everywhere! Too many major landscape processes remain only broadly dated. One change that is relatively easy to achieve is to ensure that a requirement for multiple scientific dates is in all Briefs and WSIs. Contractors compete on price but a universal requirement would create a level playing field. It would be easy to jettison or re-focus funds allocated in this way to something else if material suitable for dating is not present, but it is far more difficult (or impossible) to transfer money from other commitments to dating. (When did pottery ever get ignored, irrespective of its quality?) It is evident that there should be fairness across the board in the way that material is dealt with.

Dendroclimatological work on existing timbers (e.g. those from Carlisle and Vindolanda) should be undertaken; a pilot study would be very suitable for an undergraduate dissertation.

6.2 Large strategic excavation.

Environmental and structural questions could be addressed by a large strategic excavation: a slice through the Wall and its associated features (berm, Vallum) along with an indigenous-style settlement in its vicinity (see 4.2). Such a transect should also include land to north and south of Wall. Every available technique should be applied, thus assessing the complementarity of the information that they yield.

46. Drain under the north gate at Chesters

6.3 Sites under threat.

We should use the opportunities provided by sites under erosion; these may be a useful random check with which to test hypotheses generated from elsewhere as eroding sites are not 'chosen' for specific archaeological reasons though they may of course by happenstance fit with research questions. It is unlikely that all sites in this category can be protected from erosion and they should therefore be given priority for full investigation.

6.4 Fine-resolution pollen studies.

A network of sites would help to investigate and to illustrate the history of landscape management - and this could be tied to any strategic excavation (see 4.2 and 7.3). Any attempt to deduce fine patterns in the use of the landscape requires small bogs with a local catchment, and the area to the west of Carlisle offers great potential for this. We know that woodland continued for longer in the west and by targeting a sample of small bogs it should be possible to determine clearance patterns and whether there was any significant rural activity.

6.5 Available skills and succession planning.

The pool of skills available will largely determine what is done, whatever our aspirations. There are no geoarchaeologists in the region for example. While section morphology of the Vallum is desirable, there is no one to undertake it. Specific schemes of training will be needed (see also 7.12). Small-scale, short-term projects might be sustainable but major work will not be possible with existing staff.

Succession-planning is now also a major issue (see also VII). We must, consciously, identify the skills that we need to grow. Small focussed projects would be very appropriate for training. Material in the existing archives could be used to address specific questions, providing scope for undergraduate projects. There is an urgent need to train and mentor young people, as there is already a shortage of specialists in the north. A sustainable base of trained excavators and specialists is a fundamental prerequisite for the delivery of this framework.

47. Corbridge aqueduct

6.6 Specific biological materials.

There is a need to think more creatively about differential preservation: bone preservation is a serious problem across much of our area, but material might just survive in pockets in the central limestone areas. This could be a consideration when choosing an area for a strategic excavation and might be linked to ALSF in areas associated with previous aggregate quarries such as the area north of Chollerford.

Any new investigation must have a programme of sieving, e.g. for small mammals, fish, bird, mineralised remains, and taking recovery biases into account. Again, this should be written into the brief for any significant intervention, whatever the driver. Invertebrates: there should be a focus on anaerobic deposits (although there are funding issues).

Museum aspects: archive material offers considerable potential for further analysis using new techniques, e.g. DNA or isotopes. However, a detailed assessment of the relevant material will be required - not only what and where it is, but also the current knowledge of its dating, and its stratigraphic integrity. (The Corbridge animal bones are apparently still available, despite reports that they'd been re-buried under the A69!). Museums need to know how to store and use what they hold.

6.7 Sites.

Housesteads offers huge potential as its landscape is complex with considerable time-depth. The waterlogged/anaerobic deposits at this site are also very extensive and have received virtually no attention and so therefore are overflowing with potential. Quite a lot of the fort has already been investigated so there is considerable potential for building upon existing knowledge and re-examining the archive material. Alternatively, work on forts to the west of Carlisle should be considered.

Milecastles 29-30 (Black Carts area) - the Wall and the putatively associated native landscape may offer further scope for transect work.

West of Carlisle the Wall is relatively little known and offers high potential for non-invasive survey techniques.

The Lanercost area offers excellent documentary material and map regression work might have considerable potential.

An indigenous-style settlement must be investigated. No rural settlement with osteological material has been excavated in the vicinity of the frontier in the west.

Coring into the Vallum at regular intervals might yield an interesting pattern.

6.8 Synthesis.

Synthesis is crucial if knowledge and understanding are not to be lost. Van der Veen's work on crop husbandry (1992) represents an excellent example of how grey literature can be brought together to generate new research questions. Synthesis will also be required from the National Mapping Programme, one of the largest current projects of data-gathering.

6.9 Water management

This vital resource is little known and just one of many topics that offer rich potential for research by an individual or would be well suited to investigation by local community groups.

S.7 Production and Procurement

7.1 Publication and syntheses.
The need to address the publication backlog for the Wall has already been identified as a key requirement (V). It is felt that this is particularly relevant for supply and production, as despite the substantial progress that has been made, full study and/or publication of some assemblages is still awaited. Hoards fall into this category, with publication of some and a modern catalogue for all needed. There is also unstudied material held by units and museums and a need to evaluate this. Reassessment is also important. The use of material should be inclusive and certainly extend to early excavations, even though there were gaps in artefact collection techniques. As elsewhere, work that is currently only available as grey literature remains a concern. The need for such basic data to be disseminated was highlighted by the *Research Framework for the Study of Roman Pottery in the North of Britain* (Evans and Willis 1997, 5), but is pertinent to all material culture in the Wall zone. This raw data will not date and should be published in as much detail as is practical. If this backlog is, as it should be, cleared, the work needs to be undertaken to the highest standard possible given the date and circumstances of retrieval. Collections need to be accessible to those with a legitimate research interest.

The study and publication of the basic data is a prerequisite for the development of detailed synthetic overviews of material culture from the frontier area. Such overviews facilitate the undertaking of integrated studies of artefact data, and the Agenda identifies a particular need for syntheses of numismatics, metalworking, faunal assemblages, samian and glass. This extends to types of sites, with the NERRF underlining the need for synthetic studies of the pottery from the milecastles and turrets, and Allason-Jones noting the absence of an overview of material from military *vici* (Allason-Jones 2002, 118).

By bringing the data together, it is possible to investigate chronological and geographical differences. Divergences between the assemblages from sites of the same type between the central, eastern and western sectors may have important implications for our view of the mechanisms of supply and trade both to these regions and over time. A detailed understanding of the subject matter is essential when compiling these syntheses and so either funding needs to be sought for specialists working to current professional standards to undertake the work or provision should be made for the training of others (See also VI). While such synthetic statements invariably date in the light of new discoveries, so long as the basic data from new excavations is made available, revisions can be undertaken as necessary. Progress in both these areas is crucial to help resolve the many fundamental questions that remain about the economies of the frontier zone (7.11).

7.2 Excavation and post-excavation analyses.
Common standards for excavation strategy and post-excavation analysis of material culture and environmental indices need, if not already in existence, to be devised by the relevant specialist groups and implemented. In particular, briefs for PPG16 work should include appropriate provision for the study of these aspects. Sieving, for instance, ought to be standard for animal bones. Modern quantification of pottery assemblages is essential, while allowance for petrological and lipid analyses should be specified.

7.3 Food and diet.
This multi-disciplinary project would link with **Landscape and Environment** and bring together the work of a range of specialists who have examined different aspects of this fundamental element of life in the frontier zone. By combining and capitalising on the available (published and unpublished) environmental, artefactual, ceramic, glass, osteological and documentary evidence it will be possible both to achieve an overarching perspective of sustenance in the region, and to set this within its national context. Such an initiative would be well suited to AHRC funding and would also provide a framework in which significant progress could be made on the delivery of a range of Strategy points, including 7.4, 7.6 and 7.11.

7.4 Existing assemblages.
The potential knowledge yield from existing assemblages ought to be maximised. While significant advances have been made in the study and publication of curated material, there is still considerable scope for residue analysis of pottery and DNA analysis of skins and animal bones. Recent study of jet, torbanite and shale artefacts has demonstrated just how much can be learnt from the application of emerging scientific techniques to existing material. An extension of EDXRF analysis on Severan counterfeit *denarii* to include examples from Corbridge, Housesteads, Chesters, Newcastle, South Shields, etc. may shed important light on early-third-century activity. A broader suite of petrological analysis should be undertaken, targeting pottery, stone and tile. Stamps from the same die can now be identified on tiles and petrology would reveal whether they are made of the same clay. Trace element analysis and mass spectrometry will also give new insights into existing material. As elsewhere, if the requisite expertise is not available in the region it is worth promoting the research potential of the resource to those active in these fields outside the region (see also below).

7.5 Integrated finds databases.
The development of integrated databases holding the core data for the range of material culture present in the WHS would offer an invaluable tool for the integrated study of finds assemblages. The demonstration that a variety of finds from different sites or layers can be directly compared permits more complex questions to be asked of the material culture, permitting models for site-specific assemblages to be developed and also a real opportunity to interrogate the economies of different types of site and over time.

7.6 *Corpora*.
The creation of corpora such as Gillam's seminal study on Types of Roman coarse pottery vessels in northern Britain push forward knowledge and serve as valuable reference

and research tools. The creation of such works should be encouraged. While some could be undertaken at doctoral level, others require a greater level of experience with and knowledge of the material.

7.7 Comparative studies.
The Wall assemblages need to be placed within the context of research work both elsewhere in Britain and on other frontiers and provinces. Areas to be investigated include the extent to which units supposedly drawn from specific regions display continuities or differences with the material culture from these localities. The Wall assemblages should also be set alongside those in the south of England and Wales. In order to facilitate study on this scale, the data need to be as easily accessible as possible to researchers based both in the UK and overseas. One solution is to place the information online, as piloted by the *'Armamentarium'* project for military equipment and *http://vindolanda.csad.ox.ac.uk* for the Vindolanda tablets, another is to undertake the audit advocated in I. In all cases, the existence of such resources should be proactively promoted to those interested in the various aspects of frontier research, particularly delegates at the *International Congress of Roman Frontier Studies.*

7.8 Characterisation.
Study of production and supply would be advanced by a characterisation of coarse ceramics to use as a basis for comparison with other types of material to see if they display similar or different trends. There is also scope for a more detailed analysis of the logistics of supply.

7.9 Industrial Landscapes.
The industrial landscape remains poorly understood. The use of map regression on quarries (4.7) and full study and publication of relevant existing assemblages (7.1 and 7.4) would represent a useful first step in quantifying the scale of industrial activity. The datasets produced by the NMP may produce further avenues for exploration. The extent to which Roman exploitation of the landscape displayed continuity with preceding activity remains unknown, but would be difficult to establish as in many cases Roman work will have obliterated any traces of earlier extraction. It is possible that excavation of rural settlements (1.6) or petrology on millstones (8.7) may produce some indications. Roman exploitation of coal and lead is just as likely to have been obscured by more recent industry, although these materials do occur on Roman sites and once again petrological analysis may produce answers. Kilns are known, although in many cases it is uncertain what is produced and excavation of further kiln sites remains highly desirable. Iron is a fundamental element of production and procurement, yet until recently slag was routinely thrown away. All evidence for industrial activity must be treated as important and recorded.

7.10 Transport networks and ports.
Apart from the documentary evidence in the Vindolanda tablets, little is known about the mechanisms of moving material into and around the frontier zone. The survey recommended in 3.1 should furnish further details relating to the road network.

7.11 The economies of the Wall zone.
Inevitably this is a massive and complex topic, and far more data are required before a reliable picture of it can emerge. Nevertheless, research in a multiplicity of areas is providing important insights into aspects of it. The synthetic overviews advocated in 7.1 would assist in attempts to clarify this, while full use should also be made of the writing-tablets, which provide invaluable documentary evidence. Many questions, including the impact of the army on the local economy, require further excavation and analysis of finds both within and without the immediate frontier zone and many of the initiatives advocated elsewhere would be expected to provide data that could make a major contribution to knowledge of this theme. In particular, almost nothing is known of the non-military economy, and a greater sample of excavated indigenous-style settlements is needed if interpretations based on consumption at such sites elsewhere in the north are to be tested (see 8.2). The existing bias away from rural sites is fundamental, as if we do not have material from them, we cannot assess their contribution. As well as material culture, pollen analysis and study of the development of cord rig has considerable potential.

S.8 Life and Society

It is likely that future excavation on any scale will have important implications for our conception of life and society in the frontier zone. The projects outlined below are those that were felt to be particularly relevant to this theme, but it must be emphasised that many of the initiatives recommended elsewhere in the Strategy can make important contributions to this topic. This theme is felt to present particular opportunities for contributions by postgraduate researchers. Equally though, the relative paucity of data collected to modern standards from civilian and indigenous settlements in the WHS means that major initiatives are required if the evidence needed to test even the most basic models of social interaction is to be acquired.

48. Excavating the shrine of nymphs and genius loci at Carrawburgh

8.1 Terminology.
Attention needs to be given to developing a terminology that helps research to move beyond the binary concepts inherent in much past work (challenging oppositions such as Roman-native, military-civil, mundane-religious, male-female, etc.).

8.2 Social Interaction.
The nature of the interaction between the local population and the army and its followers, both initially and over time, is the great unanswered question pertaining to life in the frontier zone. As well as the massive military build up, it is probable that the new market attracted migrants from elsewhere in northern England, creating further social flux. Attempting to develop ways to analyse and interpret the extent and consequences of the major changes to the rhythm of life in the region is also prioritised in the NERRF.

Osteological material from the fort and extramural settlement cemeteries - once found and sampled - may provide some insight into whether members of the indigenous population lived there and also into the geographical origins of members of the military community (see 8.4 and 8.5), but ultimately if study of this key aspect is to be advanced, more detailed investigation of the indigenous 'Romano-British' style of settlement is urgently required. Given the repeated indications of an east - west divide in pre-Roman activity, any representative project would need to target sites in both regions and would be an enormous undertaking. Field-walking sites under the plough could be used to test the assumption that such settlements had little in the way of material culture, but ultimately a campaign of excavation is required to address the issue.

Full use of environmental samples would assist in determining the economy and contemporary landscape context of these settlements. It is possible that excavation would also help to resolve questions about the extent to which the indigenous population was integrated into the monetary system.

Analysis of finds should assess the degree to which hand-made pottery continued to be used on indigenous settlements.

8.3 Socio-economic trends north and south of the Wall.
The only way to address the severe chronological problems is to date scientifically a sample of rural sites, although the problems with C14 dating for Roman-period sites are a major limitation. Vindolanda and Carlisle have demonstrated the potential for dendrochronological data from waterlogged sites. Hawkhirst is identified in 3.5 as a rural site that would be well suited to excavation, while 1.7 and 3.6 would also provide valuable chronological data for rural settlement. It remains crucial for dating to be obtained if theories about the military presence stimulating a massive increase in rural settlement to support the new market are to be tested. Any opportunities to acquire data from developer-driven interventions must be seized and the recommendations in 1.5 and 7.2 would be instrumental to this.

8.4 Investigation of cemeteries.
The NERRF identifies large-scale cemetery excavations as a priority. A burial ground is famously undergoing erosion at Beckfoot (see II), providing a compelling impetus for an intervention targeting the funerary deposits there and building on work that has already been undertaken. Alternatively, a targeted research excavation could be developed, for instance, at Binchester, where a number of mausolea have recently been located. Although there is an important ethical dimension to the excavation of cemeteries that are not under threat, the potential knowledge gain is considerable and research work is justifiable so long as sufficient resources are available to ensure that the data harvest is maximised. Stable Isotope and DNA analyses would form a fundamental element of this, with the information this furnishes about multiculturalism in the Wall zone likely to have considerable contemporary resonance. Further questions to be addressed include the nature of grave furniture, whether cremation was routinely practised on site and the extent to which burial plots were marked.

As funerary traditions are often essentially conservative, there would be a clear advantage to excavating the cemetery/cemeteries at a fort where the garrisons are firmly established. This may furnish information concerning the role of ethnicity in burial as, for example, with the Pannonian connection at Brougham, Cumbria. Alongside

49. Tombstone of T Annius from Vindolanda who died in 'the British war'

the opportunity to establish the origin of the individuals buried there, any divergence in practise when garrisons changed, and whether there is continuity with funerary traditions in the regions from which the units were putatively drawn would be ascertainable. This work can build on the rich evidence for Roman inscriptions from many of the Roman forts.

Multiple cemeteries are known to have existed at a number of sites, and are probably present but not yet identified at many others. Whether these are attributable to chronological, ethnic, religious or status differences is unknown and when devising such a project allowance must be made for the possible presence of additional, unidentified burial grounds at the various fort sites. Given the possibility that specific groups were buried apart from the others, it would be highly desirable to identify and sample all of the cemeteries associated with a particular site in order to maximise the chances of achieving a representative sample of the range of people and practises present.

Such a project would benefit from being undertaken in conjunction with a project that also addressed a fort and extramural settlement, although the resources required would be considerable.

Nothing is known about the burial practices of the inhabitants of the 'indigenous-style' settlements that are believed to have remained in occupation into the Roman period. However, a major limitation is the uncertainty about where to look since many of the dead may have continued to be disposed of in ways that appear to be archaeologically invisible. The possibility that pockets suitable for the preservation of bones exist in the central sector has been identified and such areas would have an obvious advantage when seeking burial grounds. As with the forts, the information would be most useful if combined with modern excavation of the associated settlement, although given the limited instances of this in the Wall corridor, this would inevitably require a larger, more expensive project (See 8.2 and 1.6).

8.5 Target curated osteological material.

The osteological material from the Wall zone includes teeth and represents an important resource with potential for DNA and Stable Isotope analysis. Undertaking modern scientific analyses on this assemblage could complement or serve as a cheaper, though less definitive project to that outlined in 7.4. The existence of this material should be promoted to potentially interested parties, such as Bradford and Durham, and any opportunities for collaborative projects pursued.

50. An altar dedicated to Coventina by Crotus, Coventina's Well

8.6 Religion and religious landscapes.

A full synthesis of the range of religious practices conducted in the Wall zone is required. Important aspects include the impact that changes of garrison had on the range of deities worshipped in extramural settlements, if any, and the origins of the cults themselves, as well as the extent to which they were transformed in the Wall zone. The character of the deposition of objects both on and off site should also be assessed, including detailed work on 'structured deposition' on military sites, extramural settlement and at indigenous settlements. The PAS can play an important role here, providing data that can be followed up through postgraduate theses, as is underway for the material from the river at Piercebridge.

8.7 Agricultural landscapes.

The character of the pre-Roman and Roman landscape is explored elsewhere in this framework, but some targeted work might enable an enhanced interpretation of agricultural regimes across the area. A successful study of the distribution of findspots of various different types of quern has been conducted in North Yorkshire and could potentially give a very provisional indication of the density of late Iron Age and early Roman rural settlement within the frontier zone. While any such investigation suffers from a range of inherent limitations, not least the inability to date querns closely, it does offer a comparatively cheap way of devising provisional models which could then be refined through excavation and absolute dating. Does adoption of querns have implications as an indicator for the adoption of a Roman way of life?

S.9 The Post-Roman Archaeology of Hadrian's Wall AD 400-1000

The post-Roman theme faces a number of challenges that are also common to the pre-Roman. Both are important periods of transition, highlighted as regional priorities (NERRF and NWRRF), that suffer from acute chronological problems - though the post-Roman has the additional limitation of being very hard to target. There is not always a clear archaeological distinction between the latest Roman deposits and the earliest post-Roman ones (where present), and it must be remembered that this is a historical distinction rather than a cultural one. Precisely when the post-Roman transition begins remains a matter of debate with, as was noted in the Agenda, dates ranging from c. 350 to c. 410 having been proposed. There is a real need to collect more data for the post-Roman theme and it has memorably been observed that a programme of rigorous serendipity is needed! It is of course the deposits relating to this period that are the most likely to have suffered plough damage.

51. The tombstone of Brigomaglos from Vindolanda. Chesters Museum

9.1 The end of Roman military occupation

It is proposed that additional study of two key aspects associated with the military presence can provide an important insight into the changing nature of the frontier zone in the fourth and fifth centuries. In both instances understanding of the late fourth century is vital to understanding subsequent events.

9.1.1 Changing patterns of supply.

The Wall garrisons were supported by sophisticated production and supply networks that operated at a local, provincial and inter-provincial level. It is crucial to establish when production sites went out of use. Identifying changes to supply may be the best manner by which to demonstrate when the Roman military occupation of Hadrian's Wall ended. The increased sampling of environmental data means that this issue can be approached with more certainty now than in previous decades, although the nature of the evidence means that a range of analyses must be applied. Further study of the following indices can be expected to provide important data: pollen (for general picture of anthropogenic agricultural indicators at both local and regional levels); ceramic production and use (source of different wares, changes in forms, changes in production based on thin-sectioning, changes in distribution); faunal remains (changes in proportions of species, butchery practice, any physical evidence of different breeds and where from); macrobotanical (species and sourcing); increased analysis of proxy data focusing on insects and small vertebrate and invertebrate remains.

52. A column capital reused in the Willowford bridge abutment

9.1.2 Changes in structural components.

While it is widely accepted that there is a quantifiable difference in the quality of structures in the late fourth and post-Roman period, the dynamic(s) behind this remain uncertain. Particularly pertinent is the re-use or re-articulation of 'official military structures' such as *horrea* and *principia*. Conversion or demolition of a *horreum* indicates diverging methods of storage and presumably a departure from the previously favoured technique of bulk storage. It might also point to a reduction in the size of the garrisoning unit, or changes in diet. *Principia* are no longer considered sacrosanct, with evidence for the emergence of activities such as butchery and metalworking. On current dating, mostly derived from numismatics and pottery, this suggests a fundamental change in the military before the post-Roman period and it is important to emphasise that change also occurs in the Roman period. There is a need to reassess this dating evidence and use the structural evidence to test assumptions of the fourth-century occupation of the Wall derived from our interpretation of the second and third centuries. This can be used to inform models for 'the end' of not just the frontier zone, but Roman Britain itself.

9.2 Planning for post-Roman deposits.
It is crucial for the identification of post-Roman structures that the very highest standards of excavation are applied and that any future interventions in the Wall zone take into account the possible presence of late horizons prior to work commencing. Because of their generally ephemeral character, area excavation is vital to ensure recognition and interpretation of the physical remains of occupation in this period. It is not yet known how representative the current bias towards forts is and the scatter of late material along the Wall suggests that activity also occurred elsewhere. Given the lack of a diagnostic material culture, widespread absolute dating techniques must be employed, using Bayesian modelling to link cultural indicators with C14 dates.

9.3 Targeting the post-Roman.
In order to identify the post-Roman potential of sites, their latest material horizons should be assessed. Complementary to this, the NERRF advocates the re-assessment of post-Roman finds from sites such as Corbridge and Wallsend. Excavating sites more extensively where late activity is known is one way of maximising the chances of encountering late Roman deposits, and ultimately further investigation is the only way that we can add to the existing *corpus* of sites with post-Roman occupation. Size matters here, with large open area excavation rather than keyhole trenches needed to make sense of the post Roman deposits. Desirable targets would include Birdoswald, Housesteads, Vindolanda, South Shields, Risingham, Chesters, Bewcastle, Lanchester and Binchester. While this does run the risk of artificially reinforcing existing biases in the datasets towards forts, it currently represents the best chance to target this phase.

There has been little opportunity to search for post-Roman deposits in the extramural settlements and any future examination of these features must allow for the possibility that transitional-period occupation was not restricted to the area within the ramparts (see 5.2). Bathhouses also have considerable potential in this regard. Given the impossibility of generalising from the available evidence, if seeking such traces formed a major research objective, as it should do, there would be a considerable advantage in targeting the extramural settlement of a fort where details of the post-Roman occupation are already known. This would permit a more reliable examination of how any extramural occupation articulated with that within the defences.

It is equally important to allow for a possible post-Roman continuation of use of cemeteries.

Scattered third- and fourth-century coins in and around the *principia* at Carlisle and Newcastle have led to the suggestion that markets were established here. As both forts are arguably associated with a road north, the re-examination of Stagshaw near Corbridge has potential here. This was that site of a famous medieval fair and may have had a Roman predecessor.

There is an absence of material package from rural sites to complement the known fort assemblages. The urgent need for further examination of rural sites is a repeated theme of this Strategy and a number of the proposed projects (1.6, 1.7, 1.8, 3.3, 3.5, 6.11, 8.2 and 8.4) may generate important comparative material. However, as the majority of the rural settlements within the Wall corridor remain entirely undated, it is unknown whether or not there was post-Roman occupation of the archaeologically visible sites. The pollen evidence suggesting continuity in cleared areas throughout the fifth century would be consistent with continued agricultural land management and the settlement at Hawkhirst, which has produced late-fourth-century material (Simpson and Richmond 1936, 179-182), would be a strong candidate for excavation to investigate this aspect (see also 3.5). Alternatively the most pertinent recommendation is to target those sites where late layers are least likely to have been lost to erosion or the plough.

A number of undated structures that could, perhaps, be linked to this transitional period are known in the central sector and targeted excavation may provide some important indications of the nature of activity outside the forts. The milecastles and areas surrounding them may also have potential here, as the establishment of farmsteads in a number of them could suggest a continued relevance in the landscape.

9.4 Interpreting the post-Roman.
There is clear potential for very different site specific sequences or development and it remains dangerous to generalise on the existing information. A pressing need to gather more data remains, so that we can begin to address questions such as why certain sites continue. Are we seeing continuity, or reuse and reinterpretation? A range of techniques have potential to further our understanding of the post-Roman period and these should be explored.

Lanercost, Corbridge/Hexham, South Shields, Jarrow and Bewcastle would be well suited to a pilot project investigating the potential for retrogressive landscape analysis, with the 1603 survey at Lanercost giving a baseline at the end of the medieval period. Greater use of documentary sources alongside place-name analysis should also be undertaken. Given the limited extant data, the late Roman structures at Stanwix need to be published.

Pollen analysis provides a means to tease out social versus natural changes and to provide further insight into the apparent stability of cleared land through the fifth century.

Given the ephemeral nature of the post-Roman and limited quantity of data, it is crucial to look more broadly outside the Wall zone for *comparanda*. This should include sites both where occupation continues into the fifth century and where it ends around 410, so that the different stratigraphic sequences can be compared.

It is important for Romanists to collaborate with scholars studying the Early Medieval period for their perspective on this transitional period.

ACTION PLAN

Themes and priorities	Activities	Requirements and Opportunities	Outcomes	Agenda Numbers	Strategy Numbers
A) Raising profile, creating cohesion	Set up forum to provide liaison for research on Hadrian's Wall. Instigation of annual 'Hadrian's Wall Archaeology Day' and annual publication	Define membership, scope and regularity of meeting of forum. Establish regular venue, time of year, format and publicity for Archaeology Day. Organise production and format of Magazine covering recent, current and future research on the Wall.	1) High-profile, cohesive research environment. 2) Body to push for delivery of Strategy. 3) Increased archaeological activity. 4) Annual publication 5) Community involvement 6) Increased awareness at regional, national and international levels of research on Hadrian's Wall.		
B) Non-invasive survey	Geophysical survey. Aerial survey. LiDAR. Earthwork Survey. Test pitting.	Complete set of surveys for principal sites. Regular aerial reconnaissance when conditions are appropriate. Testing of results to check interpretation and establish survival of the monument.	1) Increased awareness of extent, survival, complexity and management requirements of sites and course of Wall. 2) Ability to maximise impact of future interventions.	1.1, 1.5, 1.6, 1.9, 2.1, 2.3.4, 2.4, 2.5, 2.6, 3.1, 3.5.5, 3.5.6, 3.5.8, 3.6, 4.7, 5.4	V, VI, VIII 1.1, 3.1, 3.2, 3.5, 3.6, 4.1, 4.4, 5.1
C) Recording, managing, modelling and disseminating existing data	Audit existing material. Address publication backlog. Develop GIS. Undertake modern scientific analysis of curated material. Develop web resource detailing where interventions are underway on the Wall	Detailed survey of existing material. Full publication of major excavations/assemblages. Determine scope, purpose and hosting of GIS. Assess suitability of existing assemblages for scientific analysis.	1) Showcase multi-disciplinary research potential of Wall assemblages. 2) Essential research and management tool. 3) Ability to analyse objectively important excavations. 4) Maximise knowledge output from existing material. 5) Raise awareness of where work is conducted.	2.3, 2.4, 2.5, 3.2, 5.3.5, 5.6, 6.1, 7.2,	I, III, V, VI, 3.7, 5.4, 7.1, 7.3, 7.4, 7.5, 8.5, 9.4

		Find host to create and maintain web resource.			
D) Flagship projects	Undertaking of major cross-thematic initiatives that deliver multiple Agenda items, raise the profile of Hadrian's Wall research and provide opportunities for community involvement	2 transects across the Wall, one in East and one in West. Extramural settlement excavation. Rural settlement excavation. Cemetery excavation. Food and diet. Dissemination of results at an academic and popular level.	1) Modern data benefiting from full scientific analysis. 2) Massive increase in knowledge of key aspects. 3) Demonstration of suitability of Hadrian's Wall for high-profile projects with an international significance.	1.3, 1.6, 1.8, 1.9, 2.1, 2.4, 2.5, 3.1, 3.3, 3.5.2, 3.5.3, 3.5.4, 3.5.7, 4.1, 4.6, 4.7, 4.8, 4.9, 5.2, 5.3, 5.4.2, 5.6, 6.2, 6.3, 6.4, 7.1, 7.3, 7.4, 7.5, 8.1, 8.2, 8.3, 8.4	IV, V, IX, 4.2, 5.2, 7.3, 8.4
E) Synthesis and *corpora*	Detailed synthesis of material from the Wall zone. Setting of this within national and international contexts. Creation of *corpora* for material culture.	Familiarity with material. Particular attention needed for material culture and Iron Age - Roman transition. Knowledge of the national and international context and *comparanda*.	1) Creation of valuable research and reference tools to be refined through future research. 2) Dissemination of specialist knowledge. 3) A statement of the position of Wall assemblages, structures and settlements in the wider national and international context.	1.7, 4.9, 5.1.6, 6.1, 6.2, 6.3, 6.4, 8.2.5	V, VII, 1.3, 3.5, 6.8, 7.1, 7.3, 7.6
F) Chronology	Absolute dating. Excavation. Map regression. Field walking.	Multiple scientific dates in contractor briefs. Bayesian modelling of C14 dates. Target sites for suitable samples. Community groups for map regression.	1) Maximise dating opportunities provided by archaeological interventions. 2) The fundamental data needed to begin meaningful interpretation of a wide range of landscape and settlement processes. 3) The refining of dates for the broad chronological framework that exists for the military occupation.	1.3, 1.7, 1.8, 1.9, 2.1, 2.2, 2.3, 2.6, 3.3, 3.5.8, 4.1, 4.6, 5.2, 5.6, 8.3	IV, IX, 1.5, 1.6, 1.7, 1.8, 3.3, 3.4, 3.5, 3.6, 4.1, 4.2, 4.3, 4.5, 4.7, 5.2, 6.1, 6.2, 7.9, 7.11, 8.2, 8.3, 8.4, 8.7, 9.1, 9.3

G) Risk Assessment	Analysis of risks and identification of damage to the archaeological resource from natural agencies and human activity. Dissemination of information to visitors to ensure sustainable enjoyment of the remains.	Desk-based assessment of potential risks to the archaeological resource. Identification of areas where the archaeological resource is being actively damaged. Appropriate mitigation to ensure either study or survival of archaeological features.	1) Fully informed future management of the WHS. 2) Identification of areas most at risk for more detailed monitoring. 3) Inevitable damage offset by full study of the archaeological features. 4) Dissemination of results to promote responsible behaviour by visitors		II, 6.3
H) Knowledge transfer and succession planning	Identification of specialisms to develop. Training of small finds, environmental and pottery specialists.	Funded studentships to provide introduction to these disciplines. Mentoring by experienced individuals. Training as added value to excavation projects.	1) A sustainable mechanism to ensure that knowledge is not lost. 2) Development of new specialisms in the region. 3) Continuation of existing specialisms at the same level or higher.	6.1.2	VII, 6.5
I) Pre-Roman / Roman transition	Absolute dating of Jobey sites. Excavation of indigenous-style settlement in the West. Excavation under Roman features. Testing extent of Roman impact on indigenous material culture.	Absolute dating must be obtained from a range of sites. Geophysical survey will serve to refine targets. Inclusion of field systems. Full use of environmental evidence. Pilot study of quern evidence.	1) Chronological controls with which to assess socio-economic impact of Roman occupation and test preconceptions about the dating of these structures. 2) Data from both east and west to test theories of a divergence. 3) Greater understanding of the extent to which pre-existing settlement patterns effected or were affected by Roman military dispositions.	1.3, 1.6, 1.9, 5.7.7, 6.4, 7.4	IV, IX, 1.1, 1.2, 1.5, 1.6, 1.7, 3.5, 3.6, 5.3, 6.6, 6.7, 8.2, 8.3, 8.7, 9.3
J) Late-Roman / post-Roman transition	Gather data to make a preliminary synthesis possible Area excavation.	Possibility of transitional occupation to be considered at all Wall sites prior to interventions.	1) Basic understanding of scale and nature of transitional period occupation within the Wall zone. 2) Greater chronological control	3.2.2, 5.3.3, 5.6, 5.7.8, 8.1, 8.2, 8.3, 8.4	IV, V, 5.2, 6.4, 9.1, 9.2, 9.3, 9.4

	Absolute dating. Analysis of material culture. Environmental sampling. Assessment of sites latest material horizons. Publication of Stanwix.	More data from sites where late activity is known (forts) and elsewhere to test extent of post-Roman activity. Full use of retrogressive landscape analysis and documentary sources. Fine-resolution pollen studies	for late / post-Roman changes. 3) Ability to contrast existing data from forts with that from other sites. 4) Better understanding of land management in and after the transitional period		
K) Town and country	Survey of towns and their hinterland. Publication of unpublished material from Carlisle. Fieldwalking. Excavation at Corbridge or Carlisle. Excavation at Hawkhirst. Setting of frontier towns within their national context.	Geophysical survey of Corbridge and NMP-style study of its hinterland. Fieldwalking to give provisional indication of date of hinterland features. Excavations to target the urban deposits and industrial production. Excavations at Hawkhirst to establish the occupation span and nature of settlement(s) there.	1) Greater knowledge of management requirements and archaeological details of Corbridge and Carlisle. 2) Basic understanding of the hinterland of the towns with detailed evidence for development at Hawkhirst. 3) Detailed modern data for dating the length of occupation of the towns, their economies and structural complexity.	2.3, 2.6, 3.2.2, 5.2, 5.3, 5.6, 6.2, 6.3, 6.4, 8.2.4	IV, V, 3.5, 3.6, 7.9, 8.2, 8.3, 8.7, 9.3
L) The 'Stanegate frontier'	Geophysical survey of forts and fortlets. Testing of Jones hypothesis for the 'western Stanegate'. Survey to establish more details about the road network and ensure that focus on Stanegate is proportionate to wider system.	Discussion with original excavators and trial trenching to gain new material to critically assess Jones' findings. Aerial and LiDAR survey. Trial trenching to establish chronological relationship between Stanegate road and the installations along it.	1) Analysable information for the context of the Hadrianic frontier west of Carlisle. 2) Understanding of whether the extant road was an original element. 3) Modern data for the date and purpose of the smaller structures that are fundamental to the frontier hypothesis.	2.1, 2.2, 2.3, 2.4, 2.5	IV, 3.1, 3.2, 3.3, 3.4, 3.6, 3.7

	Establishing position of the road in overall chronology. Excavation of a fortlet.	Modern excavation of a Stanegate fortlet to attempt to refine dating and purpose of these structures.	4) A suite of new data with which to critically assess the role of the Stanegate before, during and after the establishment of the Hadrianic frontier.		
M) Material Culture	Establish and implement common standards for excavation strategy and post-excavation analysis. Prepare detailed syntheses of artefact types in the Wall zone. Set these within national and international context. Develop *corpora*. Use above as the basis for multidisciplinary studies to investigate aspects such as food and diet.	Preparation of common standards, syntheses and corpora must be undertaken by specialists and should include study and, where appropriate, publication of unpublished material. While these initiatives must be led by specialists, they provide a valuable opportunity to train up successors.	1) Uniformity in excavation sampling strategies and post-ex. analysis for the classes of material culture, making assemblages directly comparable. 2) A detailed statement of the current knowledge of material culture in the frontier zone. 3) Up-to-date *corpora*, which serve as valuable research tools 4) More trained specialists 5) Developed multidisciplinary projects such as food and diet that showcase the research potential of the Wall and make a major contribution to knowledge	1.7, 3.2.2, 4.9, 5.7, 6.1, 6.2, 6.3, 6.4	7.1, 7.2, 7.3, 7.6, 7.7, 7.8, 7.11
N) Multiculturalism	Stable isotope and DNA analysis on sample of curated osteological material to test potential knowledge yield. Excavation of cemeteries at a fort with a known garrison. Full assessment of epigraphic evidence.	Gathering of material for scientific analysis. Search for ethnic markers in forts with known garrisons. Full use of epigraphic and documentary evidence to determine ethnicity.	1) Scientific data for the level of diversity in the Wall zone. 2) Ability to test objectively the implications of the epigraphic evidence. 3) Insight into whether garrisons continued to recruit from their named region.	4.3, 4.8, 7.1, 7.3, 7.4	I, 5.6, 7.4, 8.2, 8.4, 8.5
O) Human impact and climate change	Pollen sampling and absolute dating.	The identification and sampling of a network of small bogs with a local catchment.	1) The ability to detect fine patterns in landscape use over time.	1.5, 1.6, 1.7, 1.9, 5.5, 5.7.3, 5.7.4, 5.7.8	IV, 6.4, 8.7, 9.3

	Introduction of uniform standards to sample environmental indices during excavation.	Full use of environmental indices and dating evidence.	2) The acquisition of key evidence for the nature or rural activity before, during and after the Roman interlude. 3) Robust data with which to assess the Roman climate.		
P) Conceptualising the frontier	Use GIS to test theories about relationship between the Wall and the Stanegate. Critically evaluate the uniformity and role of frontier structures. Use improved knowledge of Roman structures to test or devise virtual reconstructions. Assess existing models for the function of the Wall.	Detailed contour survey for the GIS. An analytical approach that takes greater account of the differences between individual Wall structures, such as turrets, and a critical evaluation of the relative importance of uniformity and flexibility. Use of the outstanding surviving remains to test and refine existing structural reconstructions. A detailed multi-disciplinary study of material both within and beyond the frontier zone to evaluate current perceptions of function.	1) The opportunity to test with precision visual links between installations and predict the possible sites of missing installations. 2) A medium in which the implications of the course of the Wall can be clearly demonstrated. 3) A greater understanding of how the various Wall components functioned both initially and over time. 4) The greatest possible precision in reconstruction drawings and an idea of the number of different reconstructions the surviving remains can accommodate. 5) Further progress on understanding the purpose of Hadrian's Wall.	1.9, 2.5, 3.5, 4.2.8	III, 3.7, 4.1, 4.6, 4.9, 5.5
Q) Manning the Wall	Excavation of a milecastle and its surrounding area. Detailed reassessment of which units were present in which forts, and name of the fort. Evaluate and refine models for	Geophysical survey of a range of milecastle sites, followed by targeted excavation. Re-analysis of the epigraphic, documentary and structural evidence for which units were present at which fort over time.	1) Evidence for the degree and nature of extramural activity at milecastles. 2) A statement of the strengths and weaknesses of the existing evidence for resident garrisons. 3) Evidence for the everyday role of different building types within	3.5.5, 4.2, 4.3.1, 4.5.1	4.4, 4.5, 5.6, 5.7, 5.8

	the use of internal buildings. Analysis of whether it is possible to define fort *territoria*.	Detailed analysis of finds evidence from within structures such as *principia* to attempt to determine use on a room-by-room basis. Map regression and study of early ecclesiastical landholdings to investigate *territoria*.	the fort and how their structure contributes to our overall understanding of their function. 4) An insight into the extent to which fort *territoria* can be reconstructed from surviving evidence.		
R) Unravelling landscape stratigraphies	Feed NMP data and existing earthwork surveys into GIS system. Ensure excavations include field systems and other landscape features. Map regression. Testing pitting to obtain absolute dating material from Black Dyke and ascertain its relationship to the Vallum. Survey of querns from the frontier zone.	Survey of principal upstanding features. Take full advantage of strategic excavations planned along the Wall to test landscape relationships. Use of Roman features as closely datable horizons. Study of findspots and types of quern.	1) Chronological controls for a range of landscape features, including lines of demarcation. 2) A more detailed understanding of the way in which the landscape was managed over time. 3) A landscape context for the emergence and development of a frontier.	1.4, 1.5, 1.6, 1.7, 2.1, 2.3, 2.6, 3.1, 3.6, 4.4, 5.3, 5.6, 5.7.7, 8.1	I, III, 1.1.2, 1.2, 1.8, 3.1, 3.3, 3.5, 3.6, 4.2, 4.6, 4.7, 5.1, 5.3, 6.1, 6.2, 6.7, 7.9, 8.6, 8.7, 9.3, 9.4
S) Building the Wall	Detailed recording of the Width of the Wall. Map regression on quarries. Reassessment of epigraphic records. Dating and understanding transitions.	Establish a comprehensive and accurate database of Wall widths, specifying footings, offsets etc. to be available online. Train community groups to undertake map regression. Full publication and analysis of epigraphic building records.	1) A single, reliable and easily accessible resource providing the basic grammar of the Wall's construction 2) A greater understanding of precise sources of materials. 3) An appreciation of how building gangs operated and how temporary camps may relate to this.	2.5, 3.1, 3.2, 3.3, 3.4, 3.5.1, 3.5.2, 3.5.8	I, IV, V, IX, 2.7, 4.1, 4.2, 4.5, 4.7, 4.8, 4.9

	Reassessment of camps. Analysis of the course of the Wall and assessment of the priorities it displays.	Full publication of material relating to transitions and further excavation to acquire more data. Precise data to assess the intentions of the planners.	4) Knowledge of how and when basic elements of the Wall, particularly material and width, changed over time.		

Index

(1. and 2. refer to Volumes I & II. Figures in bold refer to illustrations).